MW01136128

TAROT for BEGINNERS

The Ultimate Guide to Tarot Reading

Discover the powers of witchcraft, the meanings of Tarot cards and a complete introduction to numerology and astrology

Margaret Becker

TABLE OF CONTENT

Chapter 4 – The Minor Arcana 80

Chapter 5 – Tarot Symbolism 98

Chapter 6 – Reading Pattern Meanings and Interpretations 119

No warranties of any kind are declared or implied. Readers acknowledge that the author is not engaging in the rendering of legal, financial, medical or professional advice. The content within this book has been derived from various sources. Please consult a licensed professional before attempting any techniques outlined in this book.

By reading this document, the reader agrees that under no circumstances is the author responsible for any losses, direct or indirect, that are incurred as a result of the use of information contained within this document, including, but not limited to, errors, omissions, or inaccuracies.

INTRODUCTION

Tarot readings have spiritually guided people for centuries. It is an enlightened way for a person to get a better understanding or gain more clarity on a particular situation in their life. For those wanting to learn the Tarot for themselves or to help guide others, it will also help increase one's concentration and greatly increase your spirituality.

Learning to read the Tarot can not only be exciting and fun, but also a way to tap into your own intuition. As you gain a greater insight into your cards of choice, you will find that you begin to feel them and not just understand them. Your intuition will grow and allow you to empathize with others on a deeper level as you read their cards.

Whether you are wanting to learn because you are curious or you want to help guide others or yourself, this guide has been written to help you achieve a greater understanding and insight into Cartomancy. Cartomancy is the art of Tarot Reading using a normal deck of playing cards and is one of the oldest forms of Tarot reading.

Some Tarot readers feel Cartomancy is a little harder to learn than normal Tarot cards. But, it is the basis from which the Tarot deck arose, and isn't learning the fundamentals the best place to start?

Besides, buying a deck of Tarot Cards can be a bit hard, if not a little daunting. Every seasoned Tarot reader knows that it is not just as simple as liking the illustrations on the cards, but also how you feel about the cards. They have to speak to you and connect with you or you will feel something is missing in your readings. As a beginner, choosing a normal deck of playing cards is a lot less confusing, as there are not too many symbols, characters, and illustrations to confuse you.

Once you have learned the art of Cartomancy and have fine-tuned your psyche, you will know when you are ready to venture out to a Tarot Deck. In this easy to use and follow book, I cover all the bases, from the history of Tarot through to Tarot and Astrology. Along the way, I will teach you how to do a self-reading, different card spreads and combinations, as well as how they may relate to that of a Tarot card deck.

I have, for many years, been guided by Tarot card readings and was lucky enough to find the right materials by which to learn. Through experience, I know that finding the correct guide to help you get started can be just as hard as trying to find the right deck of cards. As I have had many spiritually fulfilling years reading the cards, I want to pass along my knowledge so that you, too, may find your path through them.

Being able to properly translate the meanings of the cards as they appear and then relate them to the rest of the spread is an art that takes time, patience, and practice. There is quite a bit to learn but soon, as I said before, it will become second nature and you will start to feel the spread in relation to the situation as you interpret it.

I started reading the Tarot cards when I was at a crossroads in my life. I spent countless hours at various spiritualists, palm readers, and Tarot card readers. I found the Tarot to be the most accurate and informative of these spiritual arts. It fascinated me, and soon I found myself delving into the world of Tarot. After countless hours of research and scouring through all the authentic shops that sold the cards, I found the most beautiful deck.

It was not more than a week into my training when I realized that I was getting confused by all the illustrations on the deck. I did not quite feel my readings as I was meant to, and that is when I turned to a normal deck of cards. It was a deck that had I had for many years, and to be honest,

I am still not sure where they came from, only that they intrigued me. I found that even though reading was a little more complex than reading from a Tarot deck, I found it somehow easier to learn.

Once I had found my essence in the normal playing cards, it was a lot easier to advance to Tarot Cards. It was also a lot easier to choose my Tarot deck! I have been able to guide many people through some situations, find love, and at times a bit of peace as they gain some clarity.

Life is too short for uncertainty and not to explore your full potential. If you are even a bit curious about Tarot reading and/or what it can do for you or someone around you, now is the time to learn. I have put this guide together to help Tarot card readers at all levels become better acquainted with or brush up on their Cartomancy skills and technique.

Reading Tarot Cards have always had a stigma attached to them, as it often gets associated with the dark arts. It is because of this that a lot of people fear what the cards have to say, as they do not realize they are not meant as a prediction of the future but rather to gain an understanding of a situation or question. By learning Tarot Reading, you are joining the spiritual quest to enlighten and guide people to better understand the workings of the cards while you guide them through various difficult, confusing, and emotional times.

Now it is time for you to stop procrastinating or overthinking, get out there, and find your deck of playing cards. Then join me as I guide you through the fulfilling and exciting world of Cartomancy to discover love, success, and prosperity in your life. It is a journey of self-discovery, greater awareness, and deeper empathy for everyone as well as everything around you.

CHAPTER 1- THE HISTORY OF TAROT

There is a lot of speculation about when Tarot readings first came about. It was once thought that regular playing cards were designed from those of the Tarot Deck. But references to playing cards that date back to the thirteenth century show that this was not the case. More evidence supports the theory that the Tarot was first read with normal playing cards. There is some evidence to support that the first documented knowledge of a playing deck can be referenced some fifty years before the existence of the Tarot.

In the East, playing cards have been used since the tenth century, but they are quite different from those that were later found in Europe and the rest of the world. Not too much is known on how the name Tarot came about except the word "Tarocchi," which is Italian for playing cards and is very similar to Tarot in spelling. Tarrochi is from the Northern part of Italy and thought to have originated in the Valley of Taro River around the fifteenth century.

The traditional playing cards do bear a resemblance to what they look like today, but when they were first used in Europe, they took on many different forms. They were not only used as playing cards, but to educate. It is for this reason that the trump cards (22 Major Arcana cards as we know them today) were added to the pack as a way to teach about various animals, elements, mythology, etc. This is why they contain various images instead of numbers and suits as playing cards or the Minor Arcana do.

There were many different kinds of packs that were used for educational purposes. Some would have images on them to represent geography teachings, animals, fish, and so on. A lot of the trump cards bore figures that resembled the Pope, emperor, High Priestess, Death, etc. came under a lot of scrutiny by the church. As such, it was not long before these cards were deemed a creation of Satan in the early 1400s. They were convinced that playing cards went against the "doctrine of providence."

During the late 1500s, the church cited gambling and card gaming as "the promotion of idols and that of false Gods" for most of the commoners or middle class. The upper class still enjoyed the mystery and excitement of the Tarot, which was usually not included in the gaming bans of that century, at least for the wealthy.

One of the first mentions of Tarot card readings being used for spiritual divination was in 1781. In a book on civilization written by clergyman Antoine Court de Gebeling (who was also known to be a freemason and occult writer), he indicates that the cards held a depth of meaning that could unlock hidden information about the world and its structure. He asserted that Egyptian Priests had coded messages about their knowledge of this in them. By creating a simple, enjoyable game, it would keep this wisdom and knowledge alive through the ages.

Jean-Baptiste Alliette was the first known mystic or fortune-teller to have used Tarot cards for divination in 1783. A Paris resident, he created cards that symbolically represented various aspects of life that may be able to predict future events. These events could give guidance in love, travel, and fortune.

Alliette created the Société Littéraire des associés libres des interprètes du livre de Thot, which was the first tarot cartomancy society. He also wrote a book on cartomancy called the "Book of Thoth." He is said to have fixed the errors on Tarot cards that could lead to misinterpretation and also created the "Grand Ettielle" Tarot deck.

It was through Alliette that the rumors of how the Tarot came about started to circulate. He suggested that the Tarot was "a book of eternal medicine" and the first-ever deck was printed on gold leaves. He even went as far as to reference the Tarot as being "an account of the creation of the world."

As you delve into the history of the Tarot or become more familiar with the deck, you may come across the "Jeu de Mlle Lenormand" deck. This deck was first published in 1843 in honor of one of the most famous Tarot card readers of her time. Marie Anne Lenormand became famous amongst the wealthy as a cartomancer, and her favored deck was a Piquet pack of normal playing cards. Her name became synonymous with Tarot card readings in the circles of the upper class during her time. She was also the court confidant of Napoleon's wife, Empress Josephine.

It was Eliphas Levi who in 1856 was partly responsible for how people view the Tarot as being part of the occult. He did this by pointing out how the 22 trump cards had a direct link to the Cabala and the letters of the Hebrew alphabet. There is evidence that the occultist movements of the modern era may have arisen from a book Levi wrote, "Dogme et Rituel."

The Tarot cards from the fifteenth century were not associated with those of the cards in the 1800s that became linked to the occult. In medieval Germany, a game called Karnoffel was played with a deck of cards known to have a suit of trump cards. Although the Tarot developed separately from Karnoffel, the cards bore a remarkable likeness to each other. Of the many medieval decks that have been documented, there are only about three known packs that have survived. One of these packs are currently kept and preserved at Yale University and can be found in their Beinecke Rare Book Library.

The deck is thought to have belonged to the last duke of Milan, Filippo Maria Visconti, and is known as "The Visconti Tarot." There are only 69 cards intact in the beautiful hand-decorated pack.

Another fifteen-century Tarot deck comes from the same family and is known as the Visconti-Sforza Tarot, which was produced in the mid-1450s. This deck is divided between two different organizations who preserve them. The last known Tarot deck of that era is The Brambilla Deck and was made for the duke in the late 1440s by Bonifacio Bembo. Bembo was a well-known court painter of that era.

These decks have an innocence about them that tells of a time when man was more open to the realm of spirituality, as it was ingrained into them. Since its creation, the Tarot has taken on many forms and gone through a long era of being completely misunderstood and shunned by an ignorant society.

The reading of the Tarot, no matter the deck of choice, requires the reader to be able to interpret the cards, not just read their basic meaning. Interpreting the cards is a skill that is acquired by learning to tune into your intuition and compassion.

They are not meant as a way to predict but rather guide, suggest, and soothe the questioner while fine-tuning the reader's spirituality.

CHAPTER 2 – STRUCTURE AND NUMEROLOGY OF THE CARDS

Leonardo da Vinci was a true visionary, and one of his many talents was the ability to show how two opposites could be tangled together to create a whole, hence one of his famous quotes: "Learn how to see. Realize that everything is connected to everything else." As we continue through this guide, you will come to see how most divination arts can be tangled together to complement each other. In this chapter, we look at the structure and numerology of the cards.

Understanding the fundamentals of numer-ology makes learning how to read Tarot easier. Although the numbers or number associations of the cards are not the main part of the reading, they do give it its depth. The numbers on the Minor Arcana cards of the Tarot deck are mostly based on the same principles as those applied in numerology. Thus, when you compare the two, you find how similar their meanings are. In fact, if you apply numerology to a Tarot/Cartomancy reading, it opens it up to a whole new scope and depth.

MEANING OF NUMBERS IN NUMEROLOGY

Numerology has been around for centuries and is based on the principle that everything has a number value to it. Take pi, for instance. It can be applied to music, construction, flight, and so on. Numerology numbers can affect everything we do, from the choices we make to our romantic relationships and even our career paths. Everything has a set of numbers, and these numbers give off their own energy.

It is through understanding these energies that we can unlock various aspects of our lives, such as:

- Life choices

- Personality

- Love

- Career

- Fears

Each person has four Major Numerology Numbers which make up their Chart. They show a person's Life Path, what their Spiritual Number is, what their Karmic Number is, and what their Destiny Number is.

UNDERSTANDING THE NUMBERS IN NUMEROLOGY

In numerology, only single-digit numbers are used. Where there are double digits, they are added together to make a single digit or simplified number.

For example:

- 10 would be calculated as $1 + 0 = 1$, thus it would be read as a 1

- 14 would be calculated as $1 + 4 = 5$, thus it would be read as a 5

There are three different number types in Numerology, and they are:

- **Cardinal Numbers** – these are single-digit numbers 1 through 9

- **Master Numbers** – these are double-digit numbers 11, 22, and 33.

These three numbers are the exceptions to the double-digit rule and are read as they are. This is because they resonate on a higher level than the other numbers.

- **Eternal Number** – 0 is the eternal number that adds a life force to whatever number it appears with. It has no beginning or end and is known as the number of life itself.

TWO WAYS TO CALCULATE A PERSON'S NUMEROLOGY NUMBER(S)

There are two ways in which to calculate the Four Major Numerology numbers needed to create a person's chart.

These are calculated by:

- Using the MM/DD/YYYY date format to calculate their date of birth. For example:

    ○ Birth Date 12/01/1990

    ○ 12 = (1+2=3), 01 = (0+1=1), 1990 = (1+9+9+0=19)

    ○ 12 = (3), 01 = (1), 1990 = (1+9=10)

- 12 = (3), 01 = (1), 1990 = (1+0=1)

- 3+1+1

- 7 would be the birth number

- It is important to note that if the birth date added up to either 11, 22 or 33, it would NOT be added together as it would be a Master Number.

- Adding together their full name (first, middle, and last), by using the corresponding numbers to the letter of the alphabet, for example; a = 1, n = 5 (14 becomes 1+4). For example:

  - Abe Dan Lamb

  - Abe = (1+2+5), Dan = (4+1+14), Lamb = (12+1+13+2)

  - Abe = (8), Dan = (4+1+(1+4=5)), Lamb = ((1+2=3) +1+(1+3=4) +2)

  - Abe = (8), Dan = (4+1+5=10), Lamb= (3+1+4+2=10)

- 8, (1+0=1), (1+0=1)

- 8+1+1

- 10

- (1+0)

- 1 would be their name number

- It is important to note that if the birth date added up to either 11, 22, or 33, it would NOT be added together as it would be a Master Number.

CALCULATING THE LIFE PATH NUMBER

The Life Path Number is the most important of the Numerology numbers, as it determines a person's personality, accomplishments, emotions, and what opportunities may await them.

This is calculated using a person's birthdate in the MM/DD/YYYY format which you add up until you get to a single digit or master number (11, 22 or 33).

For example:

- 01/01/2001

- (0+1) +(0+1) +(2+0+0+1)

- 1+1+3

- Life Path Number = 4

CALCULATING THE
SPIRITUAL NUMBER

This is sometimes called your "soul number" because it refers to a person on a more spiritual or divine level. For instance, it tells if a person is a wanderer, restless, or if they are as free-spirited as the wind.

To calculate this number, a person needs to write down their entire name, using first, middle, and last. Then take out all the vowels and assign them their alphabetical number value to add up until you get to a single digit or master number (11, 22, or 33).

For example:

- Jack Adam Dunn

- a, a, a, u

- 1+1+1+(21)

- 1+1+1+(2+1)

- 1+1+1+3

- Spiritual Number = 6

CALCULATING THE KARMIC NUMBER

A person's Karmic number indicates a person's hopes and fears. It can also illuminate why they have them and what influences there are over them. Once you have a better understanding of this, a person can figure out how to overcome them.

To calculate the Karmic number, a person must lay out their full name (first, middle, and last name), then extract all the consonants and assign them their alphabetic value. These must be added up until you get to a single digit or master number (11, 22, or 33).

For example:

- Jack Adam Dunn

- J, c, k, d, m, d, n, n

- (10), (3), (11), (4), (13), (4), (14), (14)

- (1+0=1), (3), (1+1=2), (4), (1+3=4), (4), (1+4=5), (1+4=5)

- 1+3+2+4+4+4+5+5

- 28

- (2+8)

- 10

- (1+0)

- Karmic Number = 1

CALCULATING THE DESTINY NUMBER

A person's Destiny Number is what defines them and makes them different or outstanding. It reveals a person's talents and what they are capable of, which makes it a very powerful number to know, as it may even reveal hidden potential.

The Destiny number only deals in single digits, which means that even a master number has to be added together until you get to a cardinal number. For instance, 11 has to become a 2, 22 will become a 4, and 33 will equal a 6 to reveal a person's destiny.

To get the Destiny number, you have to take your full name and add each one individually until you get a single digit. Then you add all of them together until they add up to a single digit.

Example

- Jack Adam Lamb

- Jack = 10+1+3+11 = (1+0=1) +1+3+(1+1=2) = 1+1+3+2 = 7

- Adam = 1+4+1+13 = 1+4+1+ (1+3=4) = 1+4+1+4 = 10 = (1+0) = 1

- Lamb = 12+1+13+2 = (1+2=3) + 1+ (1+3=4) + 2 = 3+1+4+2 = 10 = (1+0) = 1

- 7+1+1

- Destiny Number = 9

NUMEROLOGY NUMBERS IN RELATIONS TO THE CARDS

Each number in Numerology has a unique meaning, just like each card in a Tarot reading does. They define who we are, why we do what we do, and how to change in order to become all we were meant to be. When linked with that of a Tarot reading, it adds a deeper significance to the answers we seek.

If we compare the meaning of the numbers in numerology to those of a Tarot/Cartomancy reading, we will find similarities and/or places where numerology merges into that of the cards, especially in Cartomancy, where a normal deck of playing cards is used instead of the more graphical representations of a Tarot card deck.

ZERO (0) - ETERNITY

In Numerology, 0 is a representation of choice or potential. It is an indication that a person is about to or has just begun a spiritual journey and the answers they seek should be found if guided by their intuition. It is the number of Eternity, Life Force, and oneness.

In Tarot Readings, it is mainly represented as the start of a spiritual journey or a choice that a person has to make, one that is filled with uncertainty. It can also be a warning not to be naïve, foolish, or do anything reckless, and it encourages a person to listen to their intuition.

Represented in the Tarot as:

- Tarot Cards: Major Arcana: The Fool

No Minor Arcana

- Playing Cards: The Joker (the Joker is not always used in Cartomancy)

    No Minor Arcana

ONE (ACE OR 1) – BEGINNINGS

In Numerology, 1 is the start of the Cardinal numbers which depicts the beginning, the start of something, or a strong individual who stands out in a crowd: a leader. The number 1 is ruled by the sun which has masculine energy. It shows the person's character to be ambitious, independent, stable, and strong. It has positive vibrations to it.

In the Minor Arcana, the Ace suit cards usually depict a new beginning and depending on which suit has been drawn is mostly a positive card. In the Major Arcana, the 1 is represented by the Magician who is a powerful alchemist that has the power of creation. He is a strong individual that is independent and assertive.

Represented in the Tarot as:

- Tarot Cards: Major Arcana: The Magician, Wheel of Fortune, and The Sun

Minor Arcana: The Ace (represents 1) and Ten (10) suit cards (Wands, Cups, Swords, and Pentacles)

- Playing Cards: No Major Arcana

Minor Arcana: The Ace (represents 1) and Ten (10) suit cards (Hearts, Spades, Clubs, and Diamonds)

TWO (2) – BALANCE

In Numerology, 2 is all about balance or duality. It is a number that is ruled by the moon and therefore has mostly feminine aspects to it. The 2 is our Yin and Yang number which balances out our physical and spiritual beings, which enable us to both feel and then use those emotions. It is the embodiment of our ego, intuition, our fears, our love, and joys.

In Tarot Readings, the 2 represents both a balance and/or a delay. In the Major Arcana, the 2 is represented by the High Priestess who represents a guiding force, as she is a wise woman who is at one with nature. She can also be as vindictive as she can be kind.

Represented in the Tarot as:

- Tarot Cards: Major Arcana: The High Priestess and Justice

Minor Arcana: The Number Two (2) suit cards (Wands, Cups, Swords, and Pentacles)

- Playing Cards: No Major Arcana

Minor Arcana: The Number Two (2) suit cards (Hearts, Spades, Clubs, and Diamonds)

THREE (3) – CREATIVITY AND COMMUNICATION

In Numerology, 3 is a social number, as it is aligned with communication, good luck, and creativity. Although 3 is generally a number that is associated with luck, it can also be a number that lacks direction. The characteristics of number 3 can be egotistical, flirtatious, spontaneous, and ambitious. However, they can be irresponsible and lack discipline if not pushed. Jupiter is the planet that rules number 3 and is the planet known for ambition, wisdom, and abundance.

In Tarot Readings, the number 3 is associated with things coming together and falling apart. In the Major Arcana, it is associated with The Empress, a mother figure who is fiercely protective. She is also the embodiment of success but can be cunning and is not afraid to use manipulation. The Empress also signifies abundance and warns against procrastination.

Represented in the Tarot as:

- Tarot Cards: Major Arcana: The Empress and The Hanged Man

Minor Arcana: The number Three (3) suit cards (Wands, Cups, Swords, and Pentacles)

- Playing Cards: No Major Arcana

Minor Arcana: The number Three (3) suit cards (Hearts, Spades, Clubs, and Diamonds)

FOUR (4) – SOLID AND STABLE

In Numerology, the number 4 reflects stability, control, hard work, order, and practicality. It is a strong masculine number that pushes through no matter what and without compromise to its integrity. The 4 is the founding figure of all the other cardinal numbers and is the most stable of all.

In Tarot Readings, the number 4 also means stability, good grounding, and usually reflects as someone who is completely by the book. It is the number that "when going through hell keeps right on going." In the Major Arcana, it is represented by the Emperor, who is the father figure of the Tarot; the protector, provider, and a tower of strength for all those around him.

Represented in the Tarot as:

- Tarot Cards: Major Arcana: The Emperor and Death

Minor Arcana: The number Four (4) suit cards (Wands, Cups, Swords, and Pentacles)

- Playing Cards: No Major Arcana

Minor Arcana: The number Four (4) suit cards (Hearts, Spades, Clubs, and Diamonds)

FIVE (5) – HUMANITY

In Numerology, the number 5 is the only number that is equal parts masculine and feminine. It can be a bold number that dares to be different, rises to a challenge, but can also be quite a disruptive force. The number 5 may be adaptable but only to a certain point. It is also known as the number for humanity, as most things to do with humans come in fives, such as five fingers, five toes, and five vital organs.

In Tarot Readings, the number 5 is represented by The Hierophant in the Major Arcana who is said to have control over the spiritual, mental, and physical being. In the Minor Arcana, the number 5 represents some form of disruption or disturbance in the balance of one's life either consciously or subconsciously.

Represented in the Tarot as:

- Tarot Cards: Major Arcana: The Hierophant and Temperance

Minor Arcana: The number Five (5) suit cards (Wands, Cups, Swords, and Pentacles)

- Playing Cards: No Major Arcana

Minor Arcana: The number Five (5) suit cards (Hearts, Spades, Clubs, and Diamonds)

SIX (6) – PEACE AND HARMONY

In Numerology, the number 6 is the number that brings unconditional love, sympathy, and compassion. It is the nurturer of the Cardinal numbers and is the most maternal with a strong instinct to protect. It also depicts a deep inner knowledge or wisdom and/or commitment.

In Tarot Readings, the number 6 in the Minor Arcana usually means harmony, joy, commitment, and strength in the knowledge one gets from being in tune with their inner self. In the Major Arcana, it is represented by The Lovers. This card does not only mean romance. It also means commitment, the search for enlightenment, knowledge, truth, and compassion.

Represented in the Tarot as:

- Tarot Cards: Major Arcana: The Lovers and The Devil

Minor Arcana: The Number Six (6) suit cards (Wands, Cups, Swords, and Pentacles)

- Playing Cards: No Major Arcana

Minor Arcana: The Number Six (6) suit cards (Hearts, Spades, Clubs, and Diamonds)

SEVEN (7) – MYSTICISM AND TRUTH

In Numerology, the number 7 is the most mysterious of all the Cardinal numbers. It is known as the Heavenly number, been associated with luck and good fortune, as well as mystery. The number 7 is the number that is full of magic is always on a quest for knowledge with a great thirst for the truth. Those that are governed by the number 7 are the ones that will push forward against all odds to find the truth or get to the end, no matter what.

In Tarot Readings, the number 7 is known as the number for those who are seeking the truth and will stop at nothing to get it. It is the number that indicates a change in fortune or circumstance and is a strong spiritual number. In the Major Arcana, the number 7 is represented by the Chariot, where you see a man beneath a canopy of stars riding upon a chariot whilst his clothes are adorned with figures of the universe. This displays how both the forces of Heaven and Earth drive him.

Represented in the Tarot as:

- Tarot Cards: Major Arcana: The Chariot and The Tower

Minor Arcana: The number Seven (7) suit cards (Wands, Cups, Swords, and Pentacles)

- Playing Cards: No Major Arcana

Minor Arcana: The number Seven (7) suit cards (Hearts, Spades, Clubs, and Diamonds)

EIGHT (8) – ACTION

The number 8 in numerology is the number that represents taking action and getting things moving forward. It encompasses using both the physical and spiritual to find a way forward. It reflects strength, confidence, control, and patience while showing great compassion and understanding. It is the number that thinks things through and responds rather than reacts.

In Tarot Readings, the 8 in the Minor Arcana reflects that action needs to be taken to move forward. How the action is put into practice will determine the outcome. In the Major Arcana, the 8 is represented by Strength, which is a card that resonates compassion, understanding, and to proceed with love rather than aggressively.

Represented in the Tarot as:

- Tarot Cards: Major   Arcana: Strength and The Star

Minor Arcana: The number Eight (8) suit cards (Wands, Cups, Swords, and Pentacles)

- Playing Cards: No Major Arcana

Minor Arcana: The number Eight (8) suit cards (Hearts, Spades, Clubs, and Diamonds)

NINE (9) – AWAKENING

The number 9 is the last of the Cardinal numbers and represent a person's growth up to this point. Nine is how we got to this point and who we have become both spiritually and physically. It is a completed journey into our inner self and the wisdom we have gained from it.

In Tarot Readings, the 9 indicates our growth both physically as a human being and spiritually. In the Major Arcana, 9 is represented by The Hermit who is a recluse but usually is standing alone holding a staff and a lantern. This signifies a successful quest along a tough path, but one that was conquered alone. The bright light of the lantern shows the knowledge that was gained along the way.

Represented in the Tarot as:

- Tarot Cards: Major Arcana: The Hermit and The Moon

Minor Arcana: The number Nine (9) suit cards (Wands, Cups, Swords, and Pentacles)

- Playing Cards: No Major Arcana

Minor Arcana: The number Nine (9) suit cards (Hearts, Spades, Clubs, and Diamonds)

TEN (10) – ENDING

The number 10 can also be taken as the number one and usually indicates the completion of a journey or cycle. Since a Zero makes the number it is coupled with spiritually stronger, the number 10 is made up of two powerful numbers. It marks the end of something and the beginning of something new with a potentially clean slate. This time the journey will start with confidence, optimism, and is sure to be a success due to the life lessons already learned.

In Tarot Readings, the number 10 of the Minor Arcana also signifies an ending of the old way to start again fresh, independent, and confident that this time you won't have to find your way because you know it. In the Major Arcana, it is the Wheel of Fortune card that means a change in fortune, luck, life, destiny, and Karma.

Represented in the Tarot as:

- Tarot Cards: Major   Arcana: Wheel of Fortune

Minor Arcana: The number Ten (10) suit cards (Wands, Cups, Swords, and Pentacles)

- Playing Cards: No Major Arcana

Minor Arcana: The number Ten (10) suit cards (Hearts, Spades, Clubs, and Diamonds)

ELEVEN (11) – ILLUMINATION

The number 11 is a Master number and is a highly spiritual card. It is the number that highlights our need to get in touch with our inner-self and come to trust in our intuition.

In Tarot Readings, 11 is not represented in the Minor Arcana but is in the Major Arcana by Justice, the card that seeks to balance the scale of all sides of life both physical and spiritual. It is usually read to be the same as the Number 2 cards in the Minor Arcana.

Represented in the Tarot as:

- Tarot Cards: Major Arcana: Justice

Minor Arcana: None (Wands, Cups, Swords, and Pentacles)

- Playing Cards: No Major Arcana

Minor Arcana: None (Hearts, Spades, Clubs, and Diamonds)

CHAPTER 3 – THE MAJOR ARCANA

There are usually 78 cards in a proper Tarot Card deck which are split into 2 different parts. These are the Major Arcana which consists of 22 cards and the Minor Arcana that make up the rest of the pack (56 cards).

When a card(s) from the Major Arcana appears in a reading, it is of great significance as they represent the various stages, experiences, and major influences of a person's life journey.

The Major Arcana in a spread means that it is a very important time for the person being given the reading. The amount of these cards that appear in the reading will indicate just how important a time it is.

THE CARDS OF THE MAJOR ARCANA

The Major Arcana are not numbered as the suit cards are. Instead, they are identified by the symbol, person, and/or object on the card. They do have a strict order about them which gives them an associated number which starts at 0 through to 21.

When interpreting the Major Arcana, it is good to know what their associated number is. This number can give the meaning of the card a more two-dimensional depth, giving the questioner a bit more insight into their situation.

1. THE FOOL – THE START OF SOMETHING NEW

The Fool is an idealist on the start of a spiritual journey, full of high ideals that are searching for a better future that he knows deep down inside him is possible and could be in reach. The fool embodies how every journey of self-discovery starts with that feeling that there is something more out there, but you do not always know how to find it.

Upright: There is a risk that needs to be taken to let go of the old and start something new to discover hidden talents, gain new experiences, and grow. Trust in yourself, listen to your inner voice, but don't be reckless and heed the wisdom of others.

Reversed: Something is standing in the way of progress, moving forward, or new beginnings. It could be an obstacle that has to be overcome, a person or one's self such as a mental block. Depending on the context it could indicate being reckless, taken advantage of, and lack of foresight in a new venture.

Other: The Fool is associated with the element of air; it is mainly a positive card and as the answer to a question that requires a yes or no will be a yes.

2. THE MAGICIAN – NUMBER VALUE IS 1

The Magician card focuses on a desire to try something new and or a wish for some divine intervention or good luck that would make it come about. There is a change in fortune, lifestyle and or relationships coming, but to achieve these goals it is going to take hard work and skill. The more you put in, the greater the reward will be as new aspects and adventures start to open up.

Upright: Through hard work comes great reward, and there is a new beginning in store that is linked to the individual's unique talent or skill they have to offer. The Magician usually signifies a mentally strong person that has the will, know-how, and grit to push through anything to get what they want. Success and new beginnings are near, so don't give up or be discouraged.

Reversed: If reversed, the Magician could mean that something has gone awry in the questioner's world. They will have to stop and take stock of all that has and is going on around them to figure out what changes need to be made. Outside influences have affected the natural flow of the person's life and need to be addressed before they can move on or overcome their problems.

Other: The Magician is also associated with the element of air; it is known to be a positive card and answers a question that requires a yes or no as a yes.

THE HIGH PRIESTESS – NUMBE VALUE IS 2

The High Priestess is usually flanked by the Temple of Solomon Pillars, Boaz, and Jachin on the Tarot cards. She is also mostly displayed sitting in front of the Tree of Life, adorned with the Sun cross and Moon crescent. These symbolize her as being the protector and keeper of both. She is everything that is wisdom, mystery, and knowledge while emitting pure feminine energy.

The High Priestess is a card that is about balance, intuition, and observation. It is about realizing that a person has everything they need within themselves to go forward with whatever the situation. All one has to do is to listen to their inner voice, that gut feeling that drives you and justifies what is right or wrong. But she can also be very cunning and wiley, and she is not afraid to use her femininity to get where or what she wants.

Upright: When the High Priestess appears in a reading, it means that something which seems straightforward may need a little extra look. She is a card that shows the need for self-reflection to come to terms with all the possibilities that surround a person. It is a card of intuition and knowing that everything that is needed is well within a person's grasp.

Reversed: Don't consider going against your gut instinct if it feels wrong to leave it alone or seek out the help and/or advice from someone who knows. Do not let anyone push you to make a rash decision.

Other: The element the High Priestess is associated with is water. As she is more of a card indicative of balance, she is not classed as a positive or negative card. She is a card that gives an unclear answer to a yes or no questions, as the answer may need a bit more introspection.

THE EMPRESS – NUMBER VALUE IS 3

The Empress is the motherly card that denotes fertility, fruitfulness, a time of abundance, and success. She brings about a time of transition in one's life when you feel something is missing or something needs to be done. There may be a birth or rebirth, and this is a card that shows a future with great promise, travel, and physical and spiritual growth.

Upright: The Empress is a card that shows a transition into a successful or fruitful time of life. At work, a person could be getting promoted into a leadership role or someone may need a bit of guidance. It is a time to share knowledge, wealth, and spread some good fortune or will around. She encourages a person to set free their creative side and try to communicate more openly, not keep everything bottled up inside.

Reversed: When reversed, this card can mean that there is a difficult road up ahead that one must travel. It may mean financial difficulties, tough choices, or ending a relationship that is going nowhere. It is time to take a look at your situation to see if it is internal, external, or both influences that are causing the negativity.

Other: The Empress is a card that shows a lot of positive aspects. It is associated with the element of Earth and answers yes to a question that requires a yes or no answer.

THE EMPEROR – NUMBER VALUE IS 4

The Emperor is a strong masculine card that is bold and stable. He sits upon a stone throne that is adorned with a ram's head to depict strength. He symbolizes strength, stability, and someone who knows what he wants as well as how to get it. In the Tarot, he is seen as a father figure that balances out the more feminine and motherly Empress.

Upright: When he appears in a reading, someone new, possibly an authoritative figure, is about to enter the seeker's life to change their situation for the better. He represents ambition, leadership, father-hood, and authority. He is a figure that will withstand the test of time as represented by the stone throne upon which he sits and very rarely lets anyone down. He also represents the wisdom of time and is some from whom a person can learn.

He brings about a positive change or much wished for opportunities that could lead to financial gain. It may even be a new relationship for those that are single with someone bold, dependable, stable, and strong. For those that are in a relationship, it could mean rekindling of the flame or an ending of it for someone new.

Reversed: When the Emperor appears in reverse, it could mean that someone may have too much power and be abusing it. If it is the questioner, then they may need to take a step back and reevaluate their position. Someone could be taking advantage of another person's good nature or using their situation for their gain.

Other: The Emperor is a strong positive card that is ruled by the element of fire and answers yes to a yes/no question.

THE HIEROPHANT – NUMBER VALUE IS 5

The Hierophant is sometimes called the High Priest, as he could be portrayed as such for spirituality or a pope. He is all about the spiritual aspects of life and could be the masculine counterpart to the High Priestess, although unlike the High Priestess he brings a warning that now may not be the time for changes. Instead, it is time to embark on a journey of self-discovery.

Upright: The Hierophant can be both a positive and negative force in that where money, work, and travel are concerned, now may not be the best time for a change, risky ventures/purchases, or going away. Things may not go as planned in various aspects of both your home and work life. Be prepared for delays, mishaps, and setbacks. On a positive note, they will work themselves out, especially if the seeker listens to their inner voice and does not get pushed around. In matters of the heart, the Hierophant tends to bring about positive news that will either move a current relationship forward or see an established one be as stable as can be. For single people, it could mean meeting the love of their life.

Reversed: If the Hierophant is reversed, there could be a lack of ambition in a person's life, or they may be stuck in a rut without the want or know how to get out of it. They may feel like they are not in control of their own life or destiny.

Other: Like the High Priestess, the Hierophant will give an indecisive answer to a yes/no question, as the answer may not be as simple as it should be. Unlike the High Priestess, though, where she is all about balance, the Hierophant can be both a negative and positive card depending on the situation. The ruling element to this card is earth.

THE LOVERS – NUMBER VALUE IS 6

The Lovers is not just a good card to have in a reading for love but also for balance, harmony, unexpected changes, and chance meetings. They can also have a dual meaning and are not the best card when it comes to situations regarding finances. The cards are usually drawn as Adam and Eve which can mean uncertainty/difficulty making decisions.

Upright: The Lovers are symbolic of balance, love, and harmony in all aspects of life. That there are two of them also represents duality and the prospect of having to make some choices where your heart and mind conflict. When it comes to money, the Lovers could be a warning that now is not the time to be taking risks or overspending.

For love, there is no better card to have than the Lovers as it symbolizes a great love. People in a relationship need to take heed, as there may be some conflict or un-certainty. Take some time to consider your options before making a rash decision. For single people, this card shows the promise of meeting that right someone.

Reversed: Lovers reversed warns of some-thing that is not properly balanced in a per-son's life. It could be that something has gone out of sync in a relationship, you have taken on too much responsibility at work, or people are taking you for granted. It is time to sit and take stock of what is im-portant to you concerning those around you.

Other: The Lovers is a positive card that represents harmony and is associated with the element of air. Being such a positive card, it stands to reason that as an answer to a yes/no question, the answer is going to be yes.

THE CHARIOT – NUMBER VALUE IS 7

The Chariot is driven by a Prince who stands beneath a canopy adorned with stars, and upon his head sits a crown with a sun. His chariot is usually pulled by Sphinxes, one black and one white, signifying duality. He stands with confidence and pride in all his achievements. The card represents passion, achievement, success, and willful determination.

Upright: In romance, the card may represent that the relationship has hit a difficult patch due to communication difficulties. The questioner may be feeling slightly confused and unsure about how to proceed in with a difficult situation at work. A change of attitude will go a long way, and getting in touch with your intuition can be a great guide in navigating unpleasant situations that will arise. With some goodwill and determination, events will all smooth over and work out for the best.

Reversed: The Chariot in reverse could mean that a person needs to take notice of the direction they are going in. Are they going in that direction because it is what they want to do, or are they just going that way to appease or help someone else accomplish their dreams? A person may need to get back in touch with themselves and remember their own needs, goals, and dreams.

Other: The Chariot is a positive card that is associated with the element of water and will answer as a yes to a yes/no type question.

STRENGTH – NUMBER VALUE IS 8

Strength is a card that indicates overcoming past difficulties by having taken control of the situation. It signifies courage, compassion, and inner strength that makes a person stand out as a leader and/or hero. New beginnings will come from pushing on and breaking through the barriers that held a person back.

Upright: Strength in the position of money is a really good card, although you should never take risks with your money. Look into something solid. There may just be an unexpected windfall or promotion at work that plays to the seeker's strengths. It is also a really good card to fall under relationships, as it signifies a good bond or understanding within a love relationship or friendship. In the family, it shows the strength and support of a solid family unit.

Reversed: In reverse, this card means that a person is feeling rather weak, lacks energy, and is running out of the will to muster through. There may have been a recent setback that has taken its toll and knocked down confidence. But this is just set back, and that horse needs to be got back upon, as every major success story has its share of failures.

Other: Strength is a very positive card and is associated with the element fire. It is a yes answer to any yes/no type of question.

THE HERMIT – NUMBER VALUE IS 9

The Hermit stands alone on a mountain top, a golden staff in one hand and lantern filled with light in the other. The card indicates a need for self-reflection, a time out from the constant pressures of people and the world around us. The time needed alone to heal, sort out troubles, and find the answers we need to problems so that a chapter of life can be closed to open the next one.

Upright: The Hermit shows a time in the seeker's life when they are looking for answers to a dilemma that has shaken them to the core. This may be because of a sudden loss, a relationship that has gone sour, money problems, and so on. There is a need to know what, how, and why it happened as well as if things will ever feel right again. As the Hermit stands alone on the mountain top, his staff of gold tells of good fortune, success, and great achievement, whilst his lantern of golden light shines with the wisdom and knowledge he has gained through self-discovery and finding the answer he sought through personal growth and climbing that mountain.

Reversed: In reverse, the Hermit warns not to try and run from problems or hide your head in the sand. A person may feel trapped in a bad situation with no way out and just want to hide out on their own. Don't! Push through, don't lock the world and loved ones out. While you may be hurting, not letting them in will hurt them, too. It is better to face that mountain and conquer it, no matter how tough the going may get.

Other: The Hermit signifies a want for solitude and a need to retreat from battle. It also warns against doing so and has positive aspects to the card by encouraging the seeker to move forward, push on, and know that people we love are there to help us. In a yes or no type question scenario the answer is yes, and the card is associated with the element earth.

THE WHEEL OF FORTUNE – NUMBER VALUE IS 10

The Wheel of Fortune brings about unforeseen changes and shows a desire to change the path being followed. It is an omen of things to come that are beyond a person's immediate control, as the wheel spins, leaving where it lands up to chance/fate/destiny.

Upright: Getting the Wheel of Fortune in love is not a good card to get, but in money and career it could be the start of something great to come. But you cannot just leave things up to fate and must learn to manage your money wisely. In work, it could also show a want to move onto something new. The focus of the card is on a positive outlook, change, and luck.

Reversed: Reversed, the card can mean a loss of self-discipline, control, and faith. A setback has changed a person's outlook, and now all they can see is bad Karma. Everyone can change their luck.

Other: The Wheel of Fortune is associated with the element fire and is always a yes answer to one that needs a yes/no type answer.

JUSTICE – NUMBER VALUE IS 11

Justice brings the truth along with balance, order, and karma to a reading. She balances the scales of justice weighing the truth and wields a sword to cut through to the heart of the problem.

Upright: Justice in a relationship may signify that there are hidden insecurities that need to be faced. If there has been discontent in the relationship, a compromise will have to be settled on to restore the balance to it and breathe life back into it. Money issues will soon get resolved, and some family members may require council to help put their disputes to bed.

Reversed: When Justice is in the reverse position in a reading, it may mean there is an unresolved issue that is influencing your current situation. It can also mean there is dishonesty among your social and/or family circle that will need to be to be sorted out and the responsible person brought to justice.

Other: Justice does not answer a yes/no type question with a definitive answer, as the truth has to be carefully weighed. Justice is associated with the element of water.

THE HANGED MAN NUMBER VALUE IS 12

The Hanged Man does not paint a very nice picture, as it usually shows a man hung by his foot on a cross or stone. He represents self-sacrifice, usually for a greater cause, and a re-evaluation of lifestyle choices. He is devoted to his cause enough to give up his own life.

Upright: When the Hanged Man appears in a spread, it is time to re-evaluate the things in one's life. It can mean the loss of material things to achieve a better understanding of life. It is time for the seeker's outlook on life to change and sacrifices may have to be made to move forward.

Reversed: In reverse, the Hanged Man suggests a bad choice in the past has come back to haunt the questioner. Or, they are once again at that same crossroads where they made a bad choice before. Weigh all the options carefully and if action is not needed, leave well enough alone or the same old mistakes will be repeated.

Other: The Hanged Man is associated with the element of water and is not a very positive card. If the card is drawn to answer a yes/no questions the answer will be no.

DEATH – NUMBER VALUE IS 13

Death is usually a black skeleton knight upon a white horse riding alongside a rising or setting sun. Around him are symbols of death and destruction, but the bright sun on the horizon promises the beginning of a new day.

Upright: The Death card is probably the most well known of all the Tarot cards and the most used in movies. Although it may be used in movies to have an ominous effect, the card does not necessarily mean actual death. When the card appears in a spread it signifies the ending of a cycle so the start of a new one can begin bringing change to one's life. It is a transition into a new state of phase but one that does not come without some sort of sacrifice and/or hard work. There are some areas in life where Death is not too positive, and one of these areas has to do with romance. It may be time to reconsider a relationship, or it might mean the end of one. Death could mean that a person is wanting to improve their life or start over.

Reversed: In a reading, if the Death card is reversed, it could mean that a situation that should have ended some time ago has not. It indicates that a person should stop clinging to something that has come to an end. It is time to give up and move on.

Other: If Death is drawn as an answer to a yes/no question, it will be no. The card is associated with the element of water.

TEMPERANCE – NUMBER VALUE IS 14

Temperance is a card that symbolizes an angel-like figure usually balancing two cups with a golden halo that looks like a ray of sunshine. There is a duality/balance to this card that is interpreted as self-control and abstinence. It is the card of moderation.

Upright: In matters of work and/or home, Temperance shows that we may be doing too much or pushing too hard. Life needs a balance and time needs to be spent relax-ing and having fun, too. In romance, it could mean that the relationship is not go-ing to work out or there are problems. When Temperance falls as the money card, it shows that finances will start to improve, and any debt will start to ease off.

Reversed: In reverse, this card can be a warning to slow down, as it shows a lack of self-discipline and overindulgence. This does not necessarily mean drinking and can refer to anything such as overworking to compensate for not wanting to go home. It could indicate the use of substances as a means to escape, or overspending and so on.

Other: Temperance is associated with the element of fire and will answer yes if drawn as a card to a yes/no type question.

THE DEVIL – NUMBER VALUE IS 15

The Devil is another well-known Tarot card that is drawn with the Lord of the Underworld upon his throne with a male and female captive slave. The card embodies all things spiritual and materialistic.

Upright: The Devil in a spread means temptation that can lead a person astray and end up costing more than they are willing to pay. It is a card that in most positions shows that the seeker may be feeling as if they are caged in and have a desire to experience something new. In relationships, it can signify that a relationship has gone stale or is having a lot of difficulties because one partner is always demanding more. It may be time to sit down and evaluate your situation. A person needs to ask themselves "Is it time to move on or am I being restless and ignorant?"

Reversed: The Devil in reverse can mean that something is about to change in a situation for the better. This could be less pressure, more recognition, not having to deal with bullies and instead of feeling trapped a person will have a great sense of freedom.

Other: The Devil is mostly a negative card filled with warnings about abundance and ignorance. In answer to a yes/no question the Devil always is a no. The card is associated with the element Earth.

THE TOWER – NUMBER VALUE IS 16

The Tower card is usually symbolized with some awful scene of a fiery tower being struck by lightning and people falling from it. The Tower is said to be the most negative card in the entire pack and is a card that brings about a sudden life change that one is never ready for.

Upright: If the Tower appears in the future position, it signifies a change that may cause a lot of emotional upheaval and conflict. In work there is going to be a rough patch and problems will arise, or there will be tension with work colleagues. In romance, it could be that a partner is not being honest or there will soon be a breakup. Friendships could get strained and things said in confidence might be spilled as trust is broken.

Reversed: In reverse, the Tower means that bad news will be delayed and give a person time to prepare but it is still on its way.

Other: As an extremely negative card, the Tower answers no to a yes/no question scenario and is associated with the element fire.

THE STAR – NUMBER VALUE IS 17

The Star card gives one a sense of calm and inspiration, just like seeing a blanket of stars on a clear night. It instills hope, confidence, and feeds inspiration to those who are lucky enough to draw it.

Upright: As the stars in a clear night sky tell of a calm warm evening with a promise of a bright day to come, the Star card in a reading is one that shows promise of good clear things to come. Altercations will be resolved, money problems will get sorted out, and current struggles will be overcome. New opportunities may arise at work, and now is the time to act on them. In romance, the Star means that it is a good time to iron out any difficulties that need to be discussed with a partner.

Reversed: In reverse, the Star could foretell of a rather upside-down time at work, home, and in relationships. You may have been coasting along for some time enjoying life's rich rewards, but now it is payback time. So roll up those sleeves and dust off unused skills or talent, because you are about to put them to hard work.

Other: The Star is governed by the element air and is a positive card that will answer yes if the card is drawn to a yes/no question.

THE MOON – NUMBER VALUE IS 18

The Moon in the Tarot is symbolized as a bright moon with a face in it. It represents clarity, wisdom, and assurance.

Upright: Although the Moon symbolizes clarity and wisdom, it is still a warning that one may be on the wrong path. That they are easily led astray and may be headed for disaster. Be true to yourself and choose or get back onto your path. By sorting out what it is you truly want and remembering your hopes and dreams, you will be amazed by how clear your future will seem.

Reversed: In reverse, the Moon can represent bad situations arising which one does not quite know how to deal with. There may be a lot of pressure put on a person to perform or suddenly take over the reins, and things could get quite complicated.

Other: The Moon is associated with the element water and answers no to a yes/no type question.

THE SUN– NUMBER VALUE IS 19

The Sun is the most positive card in the Tarot deck and when drawn in a spread makes the reading a happier one. It radiates joy, hope, and optimism and puts the enthusiasm back into life just like a perfect sunny day does.

Upright: The Sun in any position gives off positive vibes and a feeling of fulfillment. In the work area, it could show a very bright future with bigger job opportunities in store. In romance, it could mean that a relationship is growing and basking in the warmth of the sun's rays. In money matters, the Sun shows a promise of growth, achievement, and accumulation of wealth. But be warned, because as the Sun feeds everything on Earth, anyone who has any abundance should give back a little to those less fortunate.

Reversed: When the Sun appears in a reading in reverse, it may mean that the questioner has not been so kind to someone close to them. They may be takening unfair advantage of a situation or are being deliberately cruel to make themselves feel better. Try to avoid the storm clouds brewing with an adjustment of attitude.

Other: The Sun is associated with the element of fire and as a very positive card, as an answer to a yes/no question, it would be yes.

JUDGMENT – NUMBER VALUE IS 20

The Judgement card usually displays pictures of the dead arising to be judged, as it is a judgment day. It has a lot of Christian connotations including that of Gabriel's horn. It is a card that symbolizes choice, being honest, and owning up to mistakes.

Upright: Past actions are now catching up and there are consequences which now have to be dealt with. If Judgement appears in the future position, whatever decision or path about to be taken should have a rethink. As the relationship card, it means that any secrets or indiscretions are soon going to come to light and have to be atoned for. In general, when this card appears in a reading, it usually represents secrets being kept and that it is time to come clean and be honest.

Reversed: In reverse, Judgment warns that it is time to stop fooling yourself and change the way you treat those around you. A person's moral compass is off, and they are aware of it but choose to ignore it as they may be hitting back from their hurt and insecurities. It is time to let go, forgive, and let the wounds of the past heal. It is not fair to take it out on others.

Other: Judgement is associated with the element of fire and as a card drawn to a yes/no question will answer yes.

THE WORLD – NUMBER VALUE IS 21

As the final card in the Major Arcana, the World represents the end of the journey for the Fool. It is a card of success, great achievement, self-satisfaction, fulfillment, and personal growth.

Upright: When the World appears in a reading, it means the end of a journey and a warning to make sure one has learned from it. To take what you have learned into the new phase that is starting and not re-peat past mistakes. Expand on the suc-cesses and achievements to ensure future growth. It is about finding your destiny and purpose in life as you travel along your cho-sen path. In romance, the World means that you and your partner have come to un-derstand each other and have taken your relationship to a higher level. With regards to money matters, it is a really good card to have, as it means that money will no longer be an issue, but it is important to keep in mind past mistakes that may have caused money issues in the first place.

Reversed: If the World appears in a read-ing in reverse, there is a blockage that is stopping the end of the cycle. It is time to take a close look at personal affairs, relationships, fears, and doubts. Only once these have been resolved will this cycle be able to end and transition into the next one.

Other: The World is a card that signifies the reaching of a goal to end that cycle of one life. As such, it is mostly a positive card and if drawn as an answer to a yes/no question it will answer yes. The World is associated with the element earth.

CHAPTER 4 – THE MINOR ARCANA

There are four suits of cards in the Minor Arcana and they are numbered from Ace (1) through to 10. Each suite includes 4 court cards which are the Page, Knight, Queen, and King. In a normal playing deck, there is no Major Arcana and the face cards have a King, Queen, and Jack for each suit.

The Minor Arcana for a normal deck of cards is read much the same as it is for a Tarot Deck. Although there is a general interpretation for each suit, number, and court card, the meanings bend depending on the spread as well as the situation. For each spread, the position of the cards and the surrounding cards add more depth and dimension to the story.

When they fall with a card such as one from the Major Arcana, you will find a lot of interesting twists as to what they reveal. As nearly all of the Minor Arcana are numbered cards, when paired with numerology they can shed a lot more light on the questioner's plight, especially if you can determine their four Major Numerological Numbers.

Reading the Minor Arcana cards has a few tiers. There is the meaning of their suit, number, and in a Tarot Deck even the symbolism can be up for interpretation. Understanding these tiers and various divination tools that can influence Tarot readings is an important part of learning how to read them.

Do not panic when you see the amount of information there is to take in, as after a few readings the interpretations will start to make sense, especially when you have mastered the various spreads and understand the positioning of the cards. As I have stated before, reading the Tarot is spiritual, but there are elements of theory that need to be mastered.

THE MEANING OF THE MINOR ARCANA SUITS

In the Minor Arcana each suit has a representational meaning:

DIAMONDS (NORMAL PLAYING DECK)/ PENTACLES (TAROT DECK)

This suit is all about business, travel, money, advancement in life, and various opportunities that have to do with a person's skill/talent.

HEARTS (NORMAL PLAYING DECK)/CUPS (TAROT DECK)

The cards in this suit represent matters of the heart, the home, a person's emotional state, and friendships.

CLUBS (NORMAL PLAYING DECK)/ WANDS (TAROT DECK)

The wand suit is most commonly associated with business ventures and matters to do with power and growth. It can, however, also represent romance and love.

SPADES (NORMAL PLAYING DECK)/ SWORDS (TAROT DECK)

This suit represents the head and the heart, or in other words your emotional and intellectual sides.

COURT CARDS (NORMAL PLAYING DECK AND TAROT DECK)

- *King* – this card is an authoritative figure such as a father, boss, or someone in power. It represents stability, reliability, strength, and structure.

- *Queen* – this card is the matriarch that offers comfort, guidance, compassion, and nurturing. The Queen is a motherly type figure.

- *Page* (Tarot Deck)/*Jack* (Normal Playing Deck) – as a young princely type figure, this card represents someone who still has a lot to accomplish and is associated with moods, immaturity, and indecision but loyalty.

- *Knight* (Tarot Deck Only) – usually represent a young person between the ages of 20 to 30 that has a fire in their soul and will fight for what they want or love.

THE MEANING OF THE MINOR ARCANA CARDS

In the Minor Arcana, each suit has a representational meaning:

ACE (OR 1) – NEW CYCLE OR BEGINNINGS

The Ace (or 1) is the start of a journey. It is usually positive, as the negative connotations of the suits will soon take a turn for the better. It is the first card of the Minor Arcana and has a strength about it.

- *Diamonds/Pentacles* – Money matters, there may be a check in the mail, or a large win, promotion with a larger paycheck. It has to do with riches and/or material gains.

- *Hearts/Cups* – A new romance or friendship. It is a card of love, joy, and kinship.

- *Clubs/Wands* – Represents health or matters to do with the health of a person's finances, relationships, employment, and/or environment.

- *Spades/Swords* – There is conflict and changes brought about suddenly.

2 – BALANCE

The number two represents a balance, where one instance of a situation may seem dire but another will make up for it with good. Nature and/or Karma always seeks to balance in the circle of life.

- *Diamonds/Pentacles* – Disharmony in the workplace, dissolving of a partnership or dishonesty in a relationship.

- *Hearts/Cups* – In a relationship, it could mean an upcoming engagement or marriage. Success or achievement and commitment.

- *Clubs/Wands* – Obstacles that lead to disappointment and betrayal.

- *Spades/Swords* – A break up of a relationship/partnership/friendship. Heartache and unexpected changes.

3 – COMMUNICATION

The number 3 is a card of communication, creativity, hidden talent, but can also be some loss or things not going entirely to plan due to lack of communication.

- *Diamonds/Pentacles* – Matters concerning finances will come through legal sources. Discord amongst family members or trouble with the law.

- *Hearts/Cups* – Discuss all options before taking a risk or deciding on something.

- *Clubs/Wands* – Wealth, advancement, or success thanks to a family member.

- *Spades/Swords* – Separation due to deceit or being unfaithful. Caught in a difficult situation or feeling trapped.

4 – CONSTANCY/FOUNDATION

The number four is the foundation upon which to build a better future/situation. You have to go through certain changes to build a stronger sense of self.

- *Diamonds/Pentacles* – Sudden cash flow from an inheritance, win, or promotion.

- *Hearts/Cups* – Changes for the better, travel or a new home.

- *Clubs/Wands* – Someone is lying or keeping secrets. Broken trust and betrayal. Changes are coming that will not better but worsen a situation.

- *Spades/Swords* – Stress, anxiety caused by worry could cause health issues. Someone will break a promise which causes a rift.

5 – DISHARMONY

The number 5 usually bring disharmony and discontent, especially where family, relationships, and friends are concerned.

- *Diamonds/Pentacles* – Find a balance between family and work life to keep a harmonious family life. A promotion at work will come from hard work and skill.

- *Hearts/Cups* – Be careful when choosing who to confide in. Someone who appears to be a friend may actually be jealous or petty.

- *Clubs/Wands* – You will find help where you least expect it and do not be afraid to ask for help, your friends will support you.

- *Spades/Swords* – A turn for the worse in fortunes and the home environment.

6 – ACCORD/JOY

Six is a number that is associated with joy and harmony. The card encourages the questioner to take caution when dealing with relationships and money matters to keep inner peace.

- *Diamonds/Pentacles* – Problems at home may be caused by external influences or a jealous ex-partner.

- *Hearts/Cups* – Expect some unexpected luck and good fortune. There may be a meeting with someone from the past.

- *Clubs/Wands* – There will be financial help from work or someone close to you. If engaging in a new business venture, it will be a success.

- *Spades/Swords* – Small successes will lead to greater things, celebrate each one.

7 – SPIRITUAL/MYSTERY

Seven has always been associated with a higher/heavenly power. It is the number of mystic energies and intrigue as well as deemed a lucky one. Depending on where the cards fall, it can caution about a setback, loss, and pain or luck, success, love, and wealth.

- *Diamonds/Pentacles* – There are some setbacks ahead, but do not be disheartened, as help with come from unexpected sources.

- *Hearts/Cups* – Beware of deceit from someone close to you, as they do not have your best interests at heart.

- *Clubs/Wands* – Guard your heart and/or possessions against manipulating persons of the opposite sex.

- *Spades/Swords* – There are a lot of challenges ahead that could lead to loss and/or broken relation-ships/friendships.

8 – TRANSITION

The 8 is a card that reflects the movement of finances, relationships, and business both good and bad. It can also signify a transition from a positive situation to a negative one, obstacles in one's path, and plans that do not work out as expected.

- *Diamonds/Pentacles* – A good financial gain may be in the cards. There could be travel in the near future and/or an unexpected marriage.

- *Hearts/Cups* – Expect a heartwarming surprise invitation, gift, or visit.

- *Clubs/Wands* – Someone close harbors a lot of jealousy which will lead to problems in a relationship or business partnership.

- *Spades/Swords* – Something that may seem to be on track and working out will suddenly go awry.

9 – PROGRESS

The number 9 is a number filled with ambition, drive, success, and progress. It is a number that when positive usually means fulfillment of a wish, desire, or the realization of a dream.

- *Diamonds/Pentacles* – Do not be resistant to a change, as it will bring about a change in fortune for the better.

- *Hearts/Cups* – A surprising change in luck will see a wish fulfilled.

- *Clubs/Wands* – A change in attitude could bring about new opportunities or romance.

- *Spades/Swords* – Progress will be set back from some bad luck which could cause health issues due to extreme stress and pressure.

10 – ENDINGS/COMPLETION OF A CYCLE

The number 10 is the last numbered card in the pack and means the end of a journey/cycle. But, it is also a beginning or dawn of a new one that can bring about both positive and negative changes depending on where one currently is in their life.

- *Diamonds/Pentacles* – A cycle of bad luck and dark days are about to end as good luck finds you.

- *Hearts/Cups* – There is a sudden change in luck as good fortune befalls you and new doors open.

- *Clubs/Wands* – A financial gain sees travel and good fortune in the future.

- *Spades/Swords* – There is a lot of trouble ahead.

KING – AUTHORITY

The King is the highest authority in a monarchy and as such will represent someone of power, wealth, responsibility and in control. In a reading, the King will signify either being influenced by such a person, meeting them, or taking on a form of control/authority.

- *Diamonds/Pentacles* – Someone who is of great influence and is very wealthy.

- *Hearts/Cups* – A man who wears his heart on his sleeve and is kind to all.

- *Clubs/Wands* – Someone affectionate, honest and true.

- *Spades/Swords* – A dark figure that is ambitious and ruthless.

QUEEN – NURTURING/GUIDANCE

The Queen is the next figure in power after the King, only she is more nurturing, caring, and compassionate. If she appears in a reading it may signify that someone will look to the questioner for support or guidance or they, themselves may be seeking it.

- *Diamonds/Pentacles* – Frivolous and social, someone who is not to be trusted with a secret. Loves to be the center of attention.

- *Hearts/Cups* – A fair woman who is full of grace.

- *Clubs/Wands* – Quiet, strong, self-assured, with grace and confidence.

- *Spades/Swords* – Manipulative, cunning, and untrustworthy – the black widow.

JACK/PAGE – NAIVETY/ IMMATURITY/LOYALTY

The Page is usually depicted as a young Prince who is immature and still has a lot to learn. He can also come across as reckless and unreliable. The Page cards show that there could be something new that is not all it was intended to be and may need some work to refine it.

- *Diamonds/Pentacles* – Young, materialistic, untrustworthy, and manipulative.

- *Hearts/Cups* – A good friend with a big heart.

- *Clubs/Wands* – Youthful, full of energy but reliable and trustworthy.

- *Spades/Swords* – Not someone to rely on, although they are youthful and charming.

KNIGHT (TAROT DECK ONLY) ADVANCEMENT

The Knight is mostly drawn as a man in his mid-twenties or early thirties. He can be seen as both fiercely loyal, strong, intelligent and trustworthy as well as the exact opposite. In some suits he is seen as unreliable, manipulative, cunning, and not someone to be trusted with confidence.

- *Pentacles* – Intelligent, reliable, trustworthy, and dependable.

- *Cups* – A romantic, artistic, and loving.

- *Wands* – Opportunistic and greedy, cannot be trusted with confidence.

- *Swords* – Strong, reliable, confident, and protective. Someone you would want to go to when you need a shoulder to lean on.

REVERSED MINOR ARCANA CARDS

When starting with Tarot card readings, there are already seventy-eight different meanings to interpret, and each of those meanings has more depth depending on where they are drawn in a spread, what card they are next to, and so on.

Normal playing cards do not have an upright or reverse, as they are usually the same no matter what way the card is drawn. What does influence them are the other cards around them and where they lie in the spread. There is either a positive or negative influence, and it is this energy that will dictate the outcome of the situation.

In a Tarot deck when the cards are in reverse, the same rule applies, but you can get a bit more depth out of the reading by following these few guidelines:

- Let your intuition guide you! As I have said all along, the more you read for others, the more in-tune to your intuition you will become. As you become more intuitive, your world opens up to the emotions flowing all around you. Eventually, you will be able to tap into a person's emotions to a point where you will know the significance of why a Minor Arcana or Court Card would appear in a reversed position.

- While upright cards tell how the situation currently stands and why, a reversed card may indicate that there is room to improve or grow before moving on to the next level. Some self-awareness or discovery may be needed, as a card in reverse could tell what is blocking the way to the next stage in a person's development.

What do the other cards in the spread say about the reversed card? Most of the time, reversed cards turn up to enable the seeker to see what the outcomes of their choices may be should they tend to ignore that little voice inside. Reversed cards must be read within the context and, as you have now witnessed, there are quite a few ways to read/interpret Minor Arcana, or for that matter, Major Arcana cards.

CHAPTER 5 – TAROT SYMBOLISM

Tarot cards are alive with symbols that fill up each card. More often than not, one tends to focus more on the card's name and what it represents without realizing that each character, letter, and even color has a meaning.

There are many Tarot card decks out there, and each has its unique illustrations on them. Although the angel on one card may not be the same on another, the meaning of the angle remains so. One card may have a cross where another has a wall of rock, like in the Hangman, but the message in those symbols can be interpreted along the same lines.

When reading the Tarot, a person needs to rely on their wisdom as much as they do the wisdom that has been handed down through generations of Tarot readers (called collective wisdom). In Tarot card readings, collective wisdom incorporates all the religious and/or the more traditional meanings of the symbols, while your own personal wisdom will come together through what you learn as you develop your reading talents and increase your intuitive powers.

When you start, you will naturally rely on what you have learned or know through your life experiences. For example, if you take a look at the sun as it appears on each of the cards it has been drawn on, you will notice that there are some differences to it. Your first impression of it would be what you already know about it, for example, it is warm and represents growth, health, joy and a beautiful clear day. Using the collective meaning of the symbol, you can form your own feelings about it concerning the current situation.

If we compare the sun on the cards, we may find that it is smaller on some, only appears on the horizon meaning it is rising or setting, and may have a face on it. All these differences can change the meaning of the sun symbol for each card. For instance, the sun on the horizon may not portray the sun in bright light and may give the card a more negative meaning. If it was worn as a halo it could embody an angel of light, truth, and compassion.

The traditional meaning for the sun in all contexts is usually one of consciousness. If it is set it will mean something is coming to an end, and rising would mean a fresh or new start. Depending on where the sun is positioned it would represent energy, the skill of a more creative nature, and growth.

As you can see, there are many ways to interpret a symbol. Instead of overloading your brain by trying to learn every nuance of each one, learn to connect their collective meanings with how you feel they fit into your current reading. Let the questioner's emotions and quest guide the way you read them. Trust your intuition and let it connect with each card, the position in which they appear, the influences of the surrounding cards over it, and the guidance the seeker needs.

COLLECTIVE MEANING OF COMMON TAROT SYMBOLS

AN ANGEL

In a Tarot reading, an Angel represents spiritual thoughts and/or messages from a higher power. They indicate that we may need more guidance than we may know and to listen to our inner voices.

THE ANKH

In Egypt, the Ankh represents life. In the Tarot, it represents balance and immortality. It symbolizes that each new day will bring a new challenge, but the sun will shine again the next.

ARCH(ES)

An arch is a pathway to something, or an opening to get to where you need to go. They can also indicate that a person needs to change the direction in which they are going.

BIRD(S)

Birds represent freedom and soaring to new heights as we find our wings. They tell us that we need to free the chains that are keeping us tied to one spot, let go, and ascend to new levels. They can represent travel to far off places and newfound emotional freedom or lightheartedness.

A BLINDFOLD

When we put on a blindfold, it is to keep from seeing what is in front of us. In a reading, the meaning is just that and can represent turning a blind eye, refusing to acknowledge what is right in front of us. It can also mean we are not being too honest with ourselves and it is time to do so, or that someone is not being honest with us, is keeping secrets, or we need to look at things from another point of view. Maybe we need to look deeper within ourselves.

A BRIDGE

In life, a bridge helps join two places that were otherwise either inaccessible or hard to get to. In the Tarot card reading, bridges are there to symbolize the many ways a person has to achieve a goal or move from one cycle into another. They also symbolize closing a gap in a broken relationship and remind us not to burn our bridges, as we may need to return to that point again sometime in our lives.

A BULL (OR JUST THE HEAD OF ONE)

In a lot of cultures, the bull is a symbol of strength. Depending on the type of bull, it also represents a person's station in life, especially that of royalty. On the Tarot Cards it represents much the same, along with stability. On the negative side, it can be seen as a sign of undue resistance, stubbornness, and inability to adapt or change.

A CADUCEUS

The Caduceus was a wand that in Greek mythology that was always associated with Mercury, who was the messenger of the Gods. The wand had two snakes wound around the staff and topped off with wings. It is also a symbol a person has come to associate with anything to do with medical and/or health. In a Tarot reading, it represents the combining of two opposite or opposing forces to reach a common goal. This goal could be one of healings, material gain, etc.

A CASTLE

Everyone wants a castle, as they are symbolic of great wealth, fortitude, and power. They can also represent the achievement of goals, hopes, dreams, and desires. On the negative side, it could be that we have locked ourselves away in a fortified place surrounded by a deep moat, untouchable, unapproachable and completely closed off so as to not let anyone in.

CAT(S) OR KITTEN(S)

Cats are generally more tuned in to the forces around them than a lot of other animals. They were worshiped in Ancient Egypt and thought to have had psychic abilities. On a Tarot card, they hold a lot of mystic or spiritual meaning along with wariness and represent having to watch our backs, as there may be someone with ill intent around us.

CHAIN(S)

The most common symbolism for chains is one of being held captive against our will, which in the cards can very well mean we are slaves to our environment, situation, work, relationships and so forth. But, they also symbolize being a slave to our thoughts, having a problem with addiction, or being our own worst enemy.

A CHILD OR CHILDREN

Children appearing on a card represent nativity, simplistic point of view, innocence, hope and fresh starts/new beginnings.

They show an optimistic view of the future with the undertones of a warning. Children are influenced by their surroundings and need to be nurtured, loved, and supported to grow and achieve their full potential.

CLOUDS

Clouds have a few meanings but mainly focus on a thought or spiritual messages. They can indicate clouded judgment, impaired vision, confusing thoughts, and air-headed decisions.

DOVE

Aphrodite held doves as sacred and as such, they are a symbol of love. They are also a well-known symbol of hope, peace, and prosperity. On some of the cards, though, it can have a slightly negative connotation in that everything can fall, which is symbolized by a dove flying down towards the ground.

EAGLE/FALCON

An eagle or falcon is a symbol of rising above the norm to soar to great heights. They are birds of prey that set their sights on their goal and get it with precision, power, and elegant grace.

FLAME/FIRE

Fire or flames have many meanings, amongst which some of the most common are prosperity, passion, and in some cultures is a test of purity and faith. We need fire to make our lives warmer and light our way.

FISH

Fish live in an abundance of water and can symbolize how we live our lives. They are also creatures that are in perpetual motion, which can mean we may need to slow down or go with the flow and watch out for the tides, so we do not get left in shallow waters.

FLAG

A flag is a symbol of possession, ownership, or conquest. It represents our position in life and great changes. It could also be interpreted as a surrender or need to be humble, admit we may be in the wrong, and have to make the first move to put things right.

FLOWERS

Flowers are found on many of the cards as a symbol of one opening up to get more exposure to the light that we need to achieve our goals.

GLOBES

A globe incorporates both the world and the circle of life. It can mean a beginning and an ending as well as great achievement, conquest, and getting established. It can also mean growing a business to its full potential.

GRAPES

Grapes have been religious symbols for centuries and represent abundance, fertility, and fruitful ventures. They can also mean redemption and a transition into a better life.

HAND

Hands indicate our ability to give, receive, and also take away. It is a symbol that represents our means to connect, communicate, and are our tools by which we perform everyday tasks.

HEART

The heart is the center of what makes everything function. Without it, we would not have life and it represents love, health, happiness, and connection. It also indicates courage and strength. It is at the core of everything we do and the decisions we make. The heart can also be a warning for us to not lose sight of our feelings, wants, desires, and compassion.

HORN

The Horn can both announce a great victory and joyous occasion or imminent doom, death, or an attack. On a positive note, they are upbeat and bring cheer to all in earshot. On a negative note, they can indicate something amiss, a failure, or something going wrong like a takeover.

HORSE

The horse is a spirit animal, and most believe that they have great empathy with high intuition. Linked to all four elements, they represent courage, balance, strength, and a will to break free of any bonds to run with the wind. They can, however, get spooked easily and take flight for no reason, which indicates that one should think before making a rash decision.

KEY

We see keys as a means to unlock things such as doors, gates, locks, etc. They symbolize unlocking one's destiny, desires, and are indicative of knowledge, truth, and revealing secrets. They can also lock things, which means something may have been locked away from us or taken out of our reach, as we cannot get through a door we need to, or that we have locked ourselves away from the world.

LANTERN

The Lantern is a symbol of a wealth of knowledge and wisdom gained through time. It can burn bright or dull with time if not kept fueled. It is a light that shines brightly to reveal the truth and light our way.

INFINITY SYMBOL

The Infinity symbol is a representation of an endless loop. It is also called the lemniscate. It is the endless flow of energy, forever in a figure eight loop of motion. It shows us that we have an abundance of spirit that never runs out. We just have to tap into our energy reserves if we feel that it is depleted. In a reading, it is there to remind us that an action can have infinite consequences and to think before we act.

LIGHTNING BOLT

The Lightning Bolt is used as a symbol of the Gods in many mythologies. It is said to be sending a powerful message, one that is meant to jolt the receiver into action and take heed of it. It can also be a tool of destruction or a symbol of revenge.

LION

A lion symbolizes strength, loyalty, courage, and is fiercely protective of its pride. It can also be brutal and destroy everything in its path. It is a warning that a beast is never really tamed and to be aware of how brutal it can be.

MOON

The moon is a powerful entity that can control and influence the tides. It has power over our moods and nature. It is a symbol of life and intuition, as it controls various cycles of our life. It is a soft subtle light that can soothe and help light the darkest of nights.

MOUNTAINS

Mountains are timeless, and this is represented on the cards upon which they appear. They rise above all and make us believe we can touch the sky. They offer great achievement and a chance to conquer our fears and harness our desires. They can also symbolize solitude and contemplation.

SEA/OCEAN

The sea or ocean on a Tarot card can mean a choppy encounter or raging storm. It indicates that there is more to what we see and a lot of mysteries to uncover. It is an expanse of opportunity and can take us to great depths if we let it.

A PATH

Paths can be straight or winding and indicative of how we are traveling through our lives. If they are full of twists and turns, it may be time to re-evaluate our situation and try a different route.

PILLARS

Pillars indicate a towering strength, and when a character on a card is pictured standing between two pillars, it indicates that they have diplomacy, are excellent strategists, and are tactful. They choose to meet in the middle.

PITCHER/JUG(S)

A pitcher or jug in a reading is representative of what is going on inside of us. What are we carrying around that needs to be emptied or purified? Or, what do we need to fill our vessel with to grow physically and/or spirituality?

RAIN

Rain cleanses the earth as it washes away the dirt, relieves the scorched earth, and gives life to all that grows in the earth. It is representative of washing away all the old to start new and fresh. It can represent fertility and the passing of a bad situation.

RAM

A ram signifies strength and determination. They can be obstinate and aggressive creatures, which in the Tarot can warn against trying to barge your way through a situation and to proceed with care.

ROPES/TWINE

Ropes are synonymous with knots and symbolize being tied up in them or being restrained. The rope can be both a savior to pull us out of tough situations or it can be our downfall by which we can hang.

ROSE(S)

Roses have always been a symbol of beauty, grace, and great promise with a threat of painful thorns if we are not careful. They are also a symbol of purity and opening up of new beginnings. The rose reminds us that there is beauty all around us and can be found in even the most treacherous of places.

THE SCALE

Scales need to be balanced to obtain the perfect ingredients. They represent justice, equality, and perfect balance or harmony. They can represent a part of our life that is not working or is pulling us down.

SCROLL

Scrolls carry the words of people from bygone eras. They were a way to pass on the information and to document various events through history. They represent the transfer of knowledge, information, or something that needs to be uncovered. It is a sign that there is something that needs to be learned to get further on your journey.

SHIELD

A shield blocks us from danger and protects us in all things, even in matters of the heart. If it appears on a card in a reading, it could either mean that you are being too protective or that you may protect yourself. It could also signify that you have your guard up or someone is guarding against you.

SHIP

A ship is a symbol of going on a journey, be it a physical, spiritual, or mental one. It could also mean a voyage of discovery. It could mean you need to take stock of the cargo you are carrying, and it may be time to unload. There is smooth sailing on your journey as well as choppy seas.

SNAKE

The symbol of the snake is one of rebirth and renewal. It is also one that may suggest we need to warm up a bit. We may need to learn how to better adapt to our situation to grow and achieve our goals.

SNOW/SNOWFLAKE

Snow has a dual meaning, as being caught in a snowstorm is like being trapped in a world of quiet. As the snow falls around you, there is no sound, and you feel like you are the only person left on earth. Thus, snow means isolation or a need for isolation to appreciate the beauty of the fresh-packed virgin snow. It can be mean starting again and wiping the slate clean.

SPHINX

In Egypt, the Sphinx is a sacred guardian to all the secrets of the universe and life. A sphinx has the body of a lion and the head of a man. It was a guardian of sacred gates which one could not enter unless they could answer the riddles the Sphinx would ask of anyone who wanted to gain entrance. It is symbolic of having to find the answer to what is holding us back in life or to making tough choices or know which path to take.

STAFF

Many cards use the symbol of the staff. It represents authority, support, and new be-ginnings.

STAINED GLASS

Stained glass is an art form that goes back centuries. It was a way of giving more dimension to glass. Looking through the stained glass can give one a distorted view of the images beyond. When there is stained glass on cards in a reading, it usually means that you may not be viewing the situation correctly but seeing it through a painted view.

STAR(S)

Stars guide us, light our way, and shine light where we need it. They are said to represent souls that have left the earth and sit in the sky to twinkle and let us know we are not alone. When they appear in the reading, it may mean we need more light in our lives.

SUN

The sun is a symbol of promise. It makes us think of clear skies and smooth sailing, warmth, life, and growth. Without the sun there would be no growth or warmth around us. When it appears on a card it has a few different meanings, and it is important to notice where it is positioned and if it bears a face or not. If it is rising it means the dawn of a bright new future, while if it is setting it could mean difficulties or the end of a difficult time with the promise that it will rise again tomorrow.

SUNFLOWER(S)

Sunflowers are always associated with happiness, as they are a large bright flower with a head filled with seeds. This means they bring about fertility and abundance as well as a ray of sunshine, as their heads are always lifted towards the sun. They tell us to always hold our heads up high and turn towards the brightness and warmth of the sun.

WOLF

The wolf is a remarkably intelligent animal. They are also considered to be the gentlemen of the forest. They are loyal, protective, but also cunning and vicious when need be. They are a warning to watch your back and know where your loyalties lie. They are also a pack animal that relies upon the support and strength of their pack. The message from this is to let those around you in, as it is not a weakness to ask for help.

WREATH

The wreath was worn as a crown of the Gods as depicted in mythology. It was also an honor to be crowned with it in the first Olympic games. It symbolizes peace, prosperity, and good will. This is why it is used during Christmas time to adorn people's front doors.

VILLAGE/CITY/TOWN

If there are scenes on a Tarot card that show a village, city, or town, it indicates that a group effort is required. One may need support from others, a group, or team to reach a personal or common goal. If the city is walled (which it usually is), it symbolizes protection, comfort, and support.

CHAPTER 6 – READING PATTERN MEANINGS AND INTERPRETATIONS

There is a lot more to a Tarot Reading that just learning the meanings of the cards. As we have discussed time and again during the course of this book, there are many aspects to the art. One of the most important ones is the pattern or formation of how the cards are laid out. This is called the spread or reading pattern.

Each pattern has a meaning for the position of the card. For instance, the Celtic Cross has past, present, and future positions. Some spreads require only one card, while others may take the entire deck. The most common spreads use anything between five and up to twelve cards.

Each position of the card will hold a meaning like a position for one's family life, love life, career, and so on. Some card interpretations will change to reflect the card before them and even the one after that. For instance, if a card falls in the past position, the next two which are the present and future must be considered. This is done before an interpretation can be properly reached because of how they all influence one another.

When the cards are drawn and placed into their position, a story starts to take place, just like a plotline it is shaped by the characters that get revealed. As the story unfolds, each card will have their base meaning and then need to be reinterpreted to fit into the storyline of the cards that directly surround it.

Before you begin to do a reading, you must first take a few minutes to get acquainted with the questioner. Make them feel relaxed and then ask them what they are hoping to find out or gain from the reading. You also need to decide on whether or not you will be using reverse cards for a more detailed reading or not. You can lay the cards down face first or face up. It is a matter of choice. But, you have to decide this before you begin the spread.

One of the first spreads anyone should learn is the popular Celtic Cross, which is known to be one of the most detailed of spreads in that is covers most areas of the questioner's queries.

THE CELTIC CROSS SPREAD

This is a good spread to learn first and is a spread that is used to answer a question. It answers in detail as it deals with the situation.

QUERENT

The first card of the spread gets laid in the middle of the table. This is the card that refers to the person for whom the reading applies. It is good to note that sometimes this card maybe someone close to the person if the card does not resemble them.

SITUATION

Card two will apply to what the situation is for the querent. It is laid horizontally over card one. It will reveal what challenges lie ahead, any obstacles or roadblocks in their way and/or the path. Sometimes it will reflect a situation that the querent needs to know about rather than the one asked about.

FOUNDATION

The third card is the basis or foundation for the situation. This card gets laid directly below card one. It reflects what in the past may have caused the situation or is going to cause it. A past indiscretion may be coming back to haunt you, and now is the time to come clean or act.

PAST

Card number four is what happened in the recent past to have caused this situation and is quite often associated with the foundation card. This card gets placed directly next to card one on the left-hand side.

FUTURE

Sometimes called the outlook card, card five gives an overview of the short-term outcome for the situation at hand. It is placed directly above card one. This is the outlook that will happen should the person keep on their current path or course.

PRESENT

The sixth card is what is happening with the situation now. This card is placed on the right-hand side of the first card. This card reflects on where the person is now and what they are doing that may be causing their current situation. It must not get confused with card 2, as that card lets the questioner know about the solution.

EXTERNAL INFLUENCES

Card number seven gets placed on the right-hand side of card number 3 but not exactly next to it, rather in the middle of and just below it. This card is representative of the current external influences that are affecting or may be causing the current situation. These influences may need to be addressed before a path is chosen, as they could get in the way of moving forward.

INTERNAL INFLUENCES

The eighth card is all the questioner's internal issues (feelings/problems) that may be causing or at least affecting the situation at hand. Sometimes, a person may be holding themselves back. Fear of failure, resistance to change, insecurities, etc. can play a major role in a person's life influences. This card is placed just above card 8, to the right of card number three.

FEARS AND DESIRES

The ninth card is representative of a person's hopes, fears, desires, and dreams. It is positioned above card number eight and to the right of card number one. Sometimes it is our fear that is holding us back from our desires. Or, a person could be torn between a very tough decision. Card number nine is placed above card number eight and to the right of card number 6.

FINAL OUTCOME

The outcome is how the situation, as it stands now, will affect a person into the more distant future. The card is placed to the right of card number five and directly above card number nine.

INTERPRETING THE CARDS IN THE CELTIC CROSS SPREAD

When first we look at the Celtic cross, we read the cards in the position that they are drawn and how they relate. For instance, the Lovers in the past position could indicate someone from your past returning. But what does the card above, below, or next to it read? Each of these cards will influence this past person returning.

The present, or card number one, is surrounded by influences and most of all is covered by the challenge of the current situation. Cards seven to ten represent the staff of the cross and are the major influences over card number one.

When you read each of the cards in the cross, the first thing that jumps out is the meaning of the card, followed by the forces around it, and then each card has more depth when you start to interpret the symbols on them. As you read the cards, you will note how the symbols influence decisions, solutions, and so on not only by their meanings, but how they flow from one card to the next.

To be able to get the most out of the Celtic Cross Spread, you have to look at how it is laid out and understand how the sections make up the cross.

THE CROSS SECTION

The section that depicts the cross are the cards on the left of the spread which are numbers one through to six. This section has two parts. First is the middle of the cross which is cards number one and two which represent the querent and their current challenge/situation. Then there is a circle that surrounds the middle section of the cross and is made up of cards three, four, five, and six.

The middle of the circle can be read in a horizontal line from cards four, one, through to six. This shows how the progression of the current situation is affecting the querent as we move from the past on the left through to the present on the right.

The horizontal line that runs through the cross shows how it started/the basis for the situation starting at the bottom with card three and running through to the future.

Together, the cross section tells the story of how the subject currently feels, how they got to that point, the root cause, past events that pushed them to this point, and what a probable future outcome would be if the issue is not addressed.

THE STAFF SECTION

The staff section of the cross is the cards laid on the right in a line and cards number seven through to ten. This is where we can see what other influences surround the querent and give a better indication of how to tackle the challenges they face.

THE BIG PICTURE

Once you have broken them into the various sections and gone into the deeper nuances, it is time to join the dots to get the bigger overall picture. To do this, you have to look at the Celtic Cross spread as a whole. Here you will be able to see the opposing forces, warnings hidden in the symbols, and the path they present as well.

Once you start to read the bigger picture, you can take all you have learned from numerology through to astrology and the symbolism of the drawings on the cards into account. This will take the querent's situation to new depths and make for a more involved and accurate reading.

The reading principles of the card as we have learned in this chapter can be applied to all the various spreads, Tarot decks, and even normal play card decks. Every spread has a unique position or placement that influences the question or situation of the querent and/or what they want an answer to.

Find the parts of the spread, break them down, interpret the cards alone, and then alongside the cards that bear a direct influence on them before broadening the interpretation to include wider influences.

CHAPTER 7 – TAROT FOR YOURSELF

One way to learn is to give yourself readings, experiment with the spreads, and find which one works best for you. Although you should master one at a time, it is important to find the one that you think works best for you. Like the perfect deck, you need a spread you can relate to, feel, and read.

In this section, we are going to explore a few methods to get to know and try. Do them a few times before deciding which one to start with to master your newfound art.

PREPARATION IS THE KEY TO SUCCESS IN ALL THINGS

SETTING UP

If you are reading for others, it is advisable to get mentally prepared, clear the air, your psyche, etc. The same is true for when you do a reading for yourself, if not more so. Most of us have a mental block when looking too deep within ourselves for fear that we will not like what we find. We don't have to find it, as we all on some level know what we are hiding deep down inside of us.

Arrange your space to have the best and maximum energy flow as possible, but be sure to have it right to allow the positive in. You do not want to invite any unwanted bad luck or negative vibes.

Go for a brisk walk or do some exercise as well as spend some down time in meditation where you can contemplate what it is you are hoping to get from the cards.

GETTING STARTED AND DRAWING YOUR FIRST CARD

Give the deck a shuffle as you think about what you are wanting to ask. When you feel you are ready to draw, choose a card while keeping what you want to know on your mind.

What does the card mean to you, not in relation to your surroundings, but to you and your feelings about your question or situation?

What is the actual meaning of the card, and does it bear any significance to you or your situation?

What is the number on the card, or the number associated with the card, and what does it mean? Does the number have a message or meaning for you?

Look at all the symbols (pictures) on the card and find out what their collective meaning is. How do you interpret their meaning? Do they have any significance to you?

Take notice of the colors/coloring of the card and find out what the colors signify. Use this concerning your situation.

On a whole, what feeling do you get from the card?

Do you think this card is about you or someone close to you?

What is the first thing that caught your eye when you saw the card? Why did it catch your eye, and what do you think it means?

Now relate all you have just thought of to everything around you.

Are there any symbols, colors, or numbers that could relate to influences around you or the environment in which you are in?

How do they relate to the people in your life and what part do they play in your situation?

How does the current card relate to your current lifestyle, work life, friends, and family life?

If you could climb into the card like Alice in Wonderland going down the rabbit hole, what do you think you find in that scenario?

Who would you talk to in there?

What would you ask them or talk about?

What would you do?

Is there something you feel you need to right in the card, redraw, help, or that you would want?

Why do you think this card in particular was drawn for you, your environment, and situation?

What do you think your intuition is trying to tell you and your subconscious with this particular card?

THE PLAN OF ACTION

Once you have interpreted the card, list down what you can take away from the card.

What warnings did you feel were in the card?

What advice is the card giving you to put you on the right path?

Then think about what you would tell someone you were reading for and give yourself the same advice. Start an action plan of how you are going to go about initiating this change. Keep the action plan up to date as you go through it.

ENDING THE READING

When you end the reading, you must place the card back in the deck, completely clear your mind, and give them a shuffle before putting them safely away. This clears the cards of any residual essence from your reading.

For the first few times you do a reading, it is good practice to write it down, along with everything that you saw, the way you felt, and your interpretation of all the questions above.

Think about everything your reading gave you or meant to you.

Take action to challenge yourself and be able to confirm that the reading was able to guide you.

SOME THOUGHTS TO PONDER OVER

There are a lot of times when the cards will not show you what you want to see. Once the card is drawn, you cannot put it back and draw again. That is defeating the objective. The cards are not there to appease you or agree with you. They are there to guide, challenge, and support you.

Try not to do a reading for yourself or anyone else if you are too over-emotional, be it sad, angry, or excited. Calm down and wait until you are thinking more clearly, even if it means having to cancel a session. In an overly emotional state, you will not get a true reading, or you may be tempted to read into the spread what you want to or superimpose your situation onto another's.

There is such a thing as too much confidence, but you will also not want to lack confidence when you give a reading. Trying to learn everything about Tarot readings is not going to happen overnight and in fact, it can take years. Even then, we learn something new almost every time we do a reading. Don't panic or try to cram too much in at once, as the Tarot is so much more than just knowing the collective meanings of the cards and symbols. As I have tried to iterate throughout this book, it is about feeling the situation and understanding and forming a connection with the cards and the questioner. You are the bridge that joins the two, and it is how you interpret their situation that comes through in the readings.

Never do a reading straight after another reading, especially not for the same person. It is not going to change what is and may give false hope. If they are insistent, tell them to try again in a day or two. This includes giving readings for yourself – you can give yourself a reading each day and multiple times a day just not one directly after the other. Wait a couple of hours and ensure that you purify the cards, room, and your soul.

It is important to always be serious about your readings, as they are an important tool that is used to enlighten one's spirit. Use the guidance the cards give you to enrich your life, learn from mistakes, and make better decisions.

Tarot card reading is a creative art that not only fine tunes your intuition, but encourages your imagination and inspires the poet in your soul.

TRY OUT THE VARIOUS SPREADS

There are many Tarot Card spreads, and the only way to find the one that you are comfortable with is to give them a try. Don't force your readings. If you are not feeling it, pack it up and come back to it later. If you are battling with a spread, then it may not be for you and it is time to try another one.

Some of the Tarot card spreads can get quite complex. These are best left to attempt when you are more comfortable with the workings, meanings, and interpreting of the cards. Stick to some of the more basic ones. Below I have listed five of the spreads that I feel are best for beginners to sharpen their skills on. These, in addition to the Celtic Cross spread from Chapter 6, should be enough to get you started.

THE ONE CARD DRAW

The one card spread is usually for a yes/no answer or a more simple answer to a question.

THE THREE CARD SPREAD

This is a very basic spread with three cards drawn one at a time that represent the past, present, and future. It gives a quick overview and possible future outcome for quick, simple readings.

THE FIVE CARD SPREAD

Also called the Pentagram Spread, as it is laid out to represent the sacred Wiccan and/or Pagan pentagram. This spread may only have five cards, but it has an abundance of meaning as even the five points of the star have their own meaning. The points are representative of the Spirit (the fifth element), Earth, Water, Air, and Fire.

THE SEVEN CARD SPREAD

There are a few variations of the seven-card spread, but one of the most popular modern-day versions of them is the Horseshoe spread. The cards are laid out in the shape of a horseshoe and significantly overlap the other to show their influence on each other. This is a fairly straightforward spread to read and incorporates nearly the same aspects as the Celtic Cross does (see Chapter 6).

TWENTY-ONE CARD SPREAD

For a broad overview of a situation and when you are starting out, one of the best spreads to practice on is the Romany, or Twenty-one Card, Spread. It has a simple layout that uses twenty-one cards that are laid out from the top left from one to seven and then down three rows from left to right. This spread is a great way to learn the various cards and view how they connect, compliment, blend, or oppose each other.

CHAPTER 8 – CARD COMBINATION

Tarot cards are a journey through the psyche of the querent. It touches on their emotional state, shows where they have come from, where they currently stand, and if they stay where they are, where they will end up. As their journey unfolds in the cards, it uncovers hidden influences/forces that may be standing in their way and gives some advice on how to better the situation.

When we read, it is like we open up a magical door and get absorbed into the symbolism of the cards. Individually, the cards have so much to tell us about ourselves, our situation, family, work life, and so on. There is a lot we can read in just one card, and with a spread we get the broad picture as one card leads into the other, showing a transition from one position to the other.

By now you have realized all the ways the Tarot cards can be interpreted and read along with the wealth of meaning of each. In this chapter, we are going to look at how to interpret a few of the Major Arcana cards with those of the Minor Arcana to get a whole new interpretation as the cards combine.

There are over a few thousand card combinations, and it is going to take time to master the collective meaning of each. But, there are a few tricks a person can use to combine the card collections. As we have discussed previously in this book, card interpretation is fifty percent collective knowledge and fifty percent personal intuition.

PRACTICE MAKES PERFECT

The only way you are going to become more confident in reading and interpreting card combinations is practice, practice, practice.

Do not be afraid to take out your deck of cards, lay out spreads, take out your trusty Tarot Notebook, and jot down how you interpret various card combinations. In the next section, I have listed a few easy methods on how to interpret card combinations.

If you need a bit of clarification, visit another Tarot card reader and take note of how they interpret some combinations of cards. There are numerous informative sites on the internet that have great Tarot Card references and lay out some card combinations. There are also a lot of books on sale that a person can buy. Some of the Tarot card packs come with their own booklet to guide you.

All it takes is ten to twenty minutes per day of going through the pack and drawing the cards out in threes or twos. Look at the cards as a whole and use the below methods to interpret them as you go. Don't forget to write what you interpret down – this is your own collective Tarot card journal.

A QUICK AND EASY METHOD TO INTERPRET CARD COMBINATIONS

USE THE NUMEROLOGY OF THE CARDS

In chapter two, we discussed the importance of numerology in Tarot and that every card, even in the Major Arcana, has a number associated with it. There are a few ways these numbers can be combined or interpreted. The cards are best read from left to right when the cards are laid out next to each other.

- If both cards have the same number, that number is amplified. For instance, if they both have the number four of different suits, then the focus is on what that number represents in the Minor Arcana as well as what it represents in the suits, only it is twice as strong, like someone trying to shout it out at double the volume. This makes it very important.

- If the numbers are from one to three, then it means a beginning or fresh start. The symbols and main focus on the card will take you into more depth, while the number tells that it is only the beginning. There may even be a two, five, and eight. In order, these will represent the beginning, the middle, and near the end of an era/situation. Numbers four through to six signify the middle of the situation and seven through to ten mean nearing the end of a cycle/journey/situation.

- Numbers that are close together such as three, four, five, etc. are a good indication that cards are referring to the stages/cycles of the situation. They should be read as new beginnings/fresh starts or endings/completion/devastation.

- Numbers that are at different sides of the ruler such as a two and a nine should be read as a major change from one situation/place/circumstance to another. Depending on if the numbers are in descending or ascending order, it will depict if the situation is going to get better or worse.

- It is good practice to read the cards from both perspectives. For instance, one scenario could mean that you are up for a promotion at work. Read in the opposite direction, it could mean that you may get passed over for a promotion.

THE UNITING OF THE ARCANAS

- Two/three Minor Arcanas together usually means that whatever the situation currently is, it is only temporary. For instance, it could signify a temporary delay in travel, getting a grant, or being able to achieve your goal.

- Two/three Major Arcana together moves the reading into one with the influences of a higher power. Something bigger than us is influencing our lives, and it may be time for a bit of meditation and a journey within, a time to change direction and to listen to our gut feeling.

- The combination of a Major and Minor Arcana gives you the foundation, the probable cause, and a good sense of why the situation arose. The Major Arcana cards in this combination usually signify the foundation (what) and the cause (how), while the Minor Arcana cards will give the reason for the situation. As an example, the Hanged Man and Ace of Hearts could signify that one let down their guard for someone, they loved only to be betrayed, but they will soon meet a new love.

CONNECTING THE SYMBOLISM
OF THE CARDS

- The symbols on the cards can either complement each other, for example a bridge and a body of water/mountain could mean bridging a gap, finding a way back, or a way forward.

- If they both have the same or similar symbols, figure out what the difference is. For instance, one card could have the sun at sunset and the other at sunrise. This could mean that as one door closes, another one is going to open. The sun may be setting on the current situation, but it will rise again.

- If they do not have symbols that go together, it could be that there is a drastic change that is about to happen where nothing will be the same again.

COMBINE THE MEANINGS
OF THE CARDS

- Combining the meaning of the cards can give you a greater interpretation. For instance, the Six of Cups combined with the High Priestess could mean to trust your intuition or listen to the child within.

- There are many ways to read the meanings of the cards when joined together, and they can mean something different if the cards are in reverse or depending on if you read them from left to right or right to left.

- If you take the position of the cards, this can also affect their meaning and give another perspective to the current situation.

THE COURT CARDS IN A READING

- Court cards can be a bit confusing, as they are not really read as a situation, warning, etc. but rather as a person/personality.

- If there are two court cards together, this could be two conflicting person-alities or two people in a romantic sit-uation. Depending on the sex or strength of the characters, it could mean that one person is trying to dominate the scene.

PEOPLE

- If there is a person or image of a per-son on each card, you can use body language to interpret the card. For in-stance, if one person has their back to the other, they could signal con-flict, feeling hurt, or walking away.

- Two kings could be a struggle for power, territory, or battle for a high up position.

- A King and Queen could be two im-portant people in your life, a mother and father, for example.

COMPARE THE ELEMENTS

- There are many symbols of the elements in the cards, and they can signify different things when put together. For instance, there could be
  storm clouds on the one card but the
  sun on the other. The meaning could
  interpret that the storm will pass and
  the sun will shine again.

- A rough ocean on one card with a
  boat on calm water on the other could
  mean that a turbulent situation will
  soon calm down.

UPRIGHT/REVERSE

- You can read both cards in an upright
  position. This shows the flow of positive forces between the two cards.

- You can read both cards in a reversed
  position, which means there could be
  a lot of strife, anger, deceit, or the
  situation will get worse if things do
  not change.

- You can read one in reverse and the other upright then swap them around. This could be seen as a negative situation reversing.

CHAPTER 9 – TAROT AND ASTROLOGY

Astrology can trace its roots in civilization back to around five thousand years ago or so. Civilized man needed to map out different positions of the sun and/or phases of the moon to depict the time of year, month, and eventually the different seasons. This was important for the planting of crops and the gathering of food for the cold winter seasons.

Eventually, the seasons were broken down into the 12 months, which is also the number of zodiac figures. The months or parts of the year became known as the phases of

149

the zodiac. These became an important guide to issues that arose in the farming communities during one or many of these phases.

Like the Tarot, an astrology reading for the week, month, or year according to birth sign can be devised depending on the date and what house the moon and or sun is in.

Like numerology, astrology can add a deeper depth and dimension to a person's Tarot reading.

Having someone's star sign helps a Tarot reading, because most if not all of the Tarot cards have an astrological sign association. Star signs can be influenced by what is known as a rising sign, which is influenced by what house the moon was in at the time of birth.

One person can exhibit the traits of two signs that either work together in harmony or at war with each other. For example, a person's birth sign could be Taurus the bull, which could be stubbornly stopping them from following their more free-flowing rising sign, Pisces the fish.

Knowing elements of the zodiac allows you to bring the astrological associations that each of the cards has to life and incorporate it into the reading.

ASTROLOGY ASSOCIATIONS TO THE MAJOR ARCANA TAROT CARDS

Each Tarot card has an association and meaning with a sign of the zodiac, along with a ruling planet.

AQUARIUS
(JANUARY 20 TO FEBRUARY 18)

Tarot Association(s): The Star

Planet: Uranus

Aquarians can be quite cold, aloof, and more than a little eccentric. They are usually polite and they do not make snap judgments. Even though they are not the most emotional people, they are still very charitable and hold a lot of compassion for others.

They are driven and talented just like the Star, and they are also the water bearers of the zodiac. Both the Star card and Aquarius are symbolized by a woman bearing water and saving the earth. On the Star, the woman can be seen as having a high level of intuition. She is also a very stable person who knows what she wants and how to get it.

Just like the Star, Aquarians are talented, driven, and march to the beat of their drum. They do not conform but rather make their path through life and usually pick up a lot of followers along the way.

There is no more perfect match than this pairing, as they both represent intellect, prosperity, hope, and can be aloof with their style and sense of self. They are not ones to join a group just because everyone else has. They are the ones that would rather start and lead the group.

Aquarius and The Star, although they shine brightly, are never the main focus but rather the beauty that glows around the likes of the more dominant moon. They can be eccentric, a bit egotistical, but they help from the kindness of their hearts and give from the very depths of their soul.

PISCES (FEBRUARY 19 TO MARCH 20)

Tarot Association(s): The Moon

Planet: Uranus

Ruled by moody Uranus with the influence of the Moon Tarot card, Pisces tend to be rather moody. They can have a dozen mood swings in one day. They are not one for public displays of anything, and like the moon they can be a bit shy and like to fade into the background.

Pisces love to help others and sometimes with total disregard to their health. The Moon in the Tarot represents compassion and strength, which they willingly extend to others in need.

Like the Moon, Pisces can be a bit mysterious in that they like to keep secrets and can at times be deceptive. Pisces are deep thinkers and are quite spiritual, just like the moon.

Pisces are idealists and can sometimes be very self-righteous like the moon when depicted with a face. The Moon can lull one into a false sense of calm right before a devastating storm. Both are sensitive and like to be in control.

ARIES (MARCH 21 TO APRIL 19)

Tarot Association(s): The Emperor

Planet: Mars

Aries is the Ram in the zodiac and can be quiet fiercely protective, just like the Emperor in the Tarot. But they are also loyal, wise, and have dignity and integrity. They are the friends you want by your side during times of trouble.

Aries the Ram can be depicted as a fatherly figure like the Emperor. They like to have their flock around them. The Emperor is a symbol of good things to come in home, family, and work. The ram is a figure that can scale great heights effortlessly.

The two are similar in meaning but when read together emphasize family and kinship. They are reliable, solid, and stable figures that both like to lend a helping hand when needed.

The Emperor and Aries are both symbols of power, strength, and great wealth. This is not necessarily material wealth but that of the spirit. They are a force to be reckoned with and mean that a situation that seemed impossible irons itself out amicably.

TAURUS (APRIL 20 TO MAY 20)

Tarot Association(s): The Hierophant

Planet: Venus

Taurus is symbolized by the bull and is stubborn, strong, and protective. They will plow through anything to protect those they love. Like the Hierophant, they have a lot of wisdom to offer and draw their strength from within them. They are very intuitive and will stop at nothing to get at the truth.

The Hierophant is a knowledgeable person who is a teacher and philosopher; a man of great spirituality who is in touch with higher powers. He, like the bull, is a traditionalist and likes to stick to the old school ways. The message they bring is to stick to the tried and trusted methods right now instead of trying something new.

Both the Taurus and the Hierophant like to collect things and keep then close. They can be very old school, preferring a more traditional or conservative approach to life. It may be time to let go a little, to relax and have some fun, or be able to move on.

GEMINI (MAY 21 TO JUNE 20)

Tarot Association(s): The Lovers

Planet: Mercury

The Gemini is said to have a dual personality being a set of twins, Castor and Pollux. These celestial twins were half-brothers with the same mother but different fathers. Pollux's father was Zeus and Castor's father was a mortal. When Castor died, Pollux asked Zeus to share his immortality with his brother which earned them a place in the stars as the constellation Gemini.

The Lovers is the card that is associated with Gemini and like the sign has a sense of duality. As there are two of them, they tend to want to go in opposite directions.

Decisions are not their strong point, and they will often just walk away rather than pick a side.

Moral high ground is not one of these people's better qualities. They are also inquisitive, free spirited, and love to communicate. The Lovers card warns that you should not just jump in feet first at the moment but rather take a step back, mull it over, or even seek advice.

Gemini and the Lovers are signs of duality, indecision, and overcommitment. As they are not able to make quick decisive choices, they tend to overcommit. But, they also remind us of fun, laughter, enjoyment like children full of curiosity, and a promise of great intellect.

CANCER (JUNE 21 TO JULY 22)

Tarot Association(s): The Chariot

Planet/Celestial Body: Moon

Cancer is the sign of the crab in the zodiac and they carry their house with them, so they are quite a mobile sign. They like to move and will shy away from conflict, rather withdrawing to the safety of their shell.

The Chariot's likeness to the crab comes in exceptional focus and mental prowess that they both symbolize. The Chariot is also a mobile card which means movement, and since two horses are pulling the chariot it means there are a few paths that can be taken. The Chariot will do its best to avoid conflict, preferring the moral high ground, whereas the Cancer will rather seek the safety and security of their warm cozy shell.

Both the crab and the Chariot are symbols of overcoming the obstacles and doing what it takes to get to where they want to go. They are both steady signs but have restless souls, and they tend to put others first.

Together they are symbolic of constant movement, non-committal, introvertedness, and a need to keep everything to themselves, including emotions.

LEO (JULY 23 TO AUGUST 22)

Tarot Association(s): Strength

Planet/Celestial Body: Sun

Leo is the lion in astrology and is the symbol of strength, the king, father, fiercely protective and a bit dangerous or unpredictable. The lion is also courageous and not afraid to take on a challenge. They are family orientated and take great pride in their family's accomplishments.

Strength is the Tarot card that is associated with Leo. Like Leo, Strength represents courage, will, and intelligence. Strength is also a card that is kind, compassionate, and giving.

When a person draws Strength in the cards, it is as a sign that they will soon have the fortitude to overcome the obstacles that are keeping them from their goals.

Leo and Strength are the champions amongst the zodiac and Tarot. They offer strength, protection, and take pride in their family unit. They are also compassionate and sturdy, pushing us forward against all odds.

VIRGO
(AUGUST 23 TO SEPTEMBER 22)

Tarot Association(s): The Hermit

Planet: Mercury

Virgo's have inner wisdom and are fiercely loyal to those that they love. They are associated with The Hermit in the Tarot, which is an excellent pairing as they both need to shut down from the world to regroup and reassess.

The Hermit likes to do a lot of introspection and will often retreat within to do so. The Hermit is usually drawn holding a lantern with glowing golden light which represents his wealth of knowledge and wisdom gained from all he has overcome and conquered.

When he appears, it means it is time to push ahead and conquer those demons by looking inside yourself to do so. Let your inner wisdom guide you and tap into your childhood intuition.

Virgo and the Hermit are the wise souls of the zodiac and Tarot. They shy away from society at times to regroup and get back in touch with their inner child and focused intuition.

LIBRA
(SEPTEMBER 23 TO OCTOBER 22)

Tarot Association(s): Justice

Planet: Venus

Libra is the sign of balance and they can be a little bit judgmental, too. They like to weigh up all the pros and cons before moving forward. Sometimes they can be a bit too overly cautious in matters of the heart, work, and making decisions.

Justice is the Tarot card that is associated with Libra and is a perfect one. They are both all about balance and weighing up the scales of truth and justice. Justice can also warn about being too overly cautious, because you could just miss the boat while you are weighing your options.

Justice can be a sign of indecision and can warn about being too judgmental or jumping to conclusions.

Justice and Libra are two peas in a well-balanced, non-discriminative pod. They bring justice to indiscretion and uncover hidden truths.

SCORPIO
(OCTOBER 23 TO NOVEMBER 21)

Tarot Association(s): Death

Planet: Mars

Scorpio is associated with the Tarot card because they are both signs of transition from one situation and/or form to another. They are both spiritual signs that are in touch with their intuition.

They are adaptable and come across as cold, aloof, and overbearing because of their intense nature. Like Death, Scorpios can be mysterious, as they keep their emotions and thoughts close to their chest. If there is a sign that you would want as a port in a storm, it would be Scorpio, as even though they are not overly communicative they are strong, reliable, and dependable.

Scorpio and Death together are both lightness and dark. They can appear to be deceptive and secretive but are strong, stable, and reliable.

SAGITTARIUS
(NOVEMBER 22 TO DECEMBER 21)

Tarot Association(s): Temperance

Planet: Jupiter

Sagittarius is a sign that follows their heart and finds balance in all that they do. Their compassion for those around them shines through them like a golden light. It is a sign that embodies the feminine spirit as they are gentle, kind, and they have a very diplomatic way of working things out.

Temperance is the Tarot card that is associated with this zodiac sign. It represents balance and communication. Temperance seeks the best path forward with the least resistance. It is a card that tells the questioner that it is time to give back, have patience, and show compassion. There must be a balance between material gain and generosity.

Together, Temperance and Sagittarius leave you feeling lighthearted, inspired, cared for and encouraged.

CAPRICORN
(DECEMBER 22 TO JANUARY 19)

Tarot Association(s): The Devil

Planet: Saturn

Capricorns are passionate people that can be very judgmental, mistrusting, and will cut anyone out of their life that has wronged them. They do not give second chances and are set in their ways. They tend to be frugal with their finances and hate waste or overspending of any kind. They can be quite negative and tend to see the glass as half empty.

The Devil is the card that is associated with Capricorn and is full of shadows and promises that always come with a price. It also means that it is time to rethink values and stop hiding away. Step into the light and embrace all the opportunities that come your way.

Together the Devil and Capricorn embody selfishness, self-righteousness, and are materialistic with a negative outlook.

ASTROLOGY ASSOCIATIONS TO THE MINOR ARCANA TAROT CARDS

The Minor Arcana are also linked to that of the zodiac.

ACE OF WAND

There is no astrological association. This card is associated with the element of fire.

When we think of the Ace of Wands, we think of will power, artistic expression, and enthusiasm.

TWO OF WANDS

Mars in the house of Aries.

This initiates a change from a rash or impulsive decision. It warns of impending dissatisfaction with a situation and to choose wisely.

THREE OF WANDS

The Sun in the house of Aries means it is time to be a little more discerning with money. There are great challenges ahead and impatience can cause a person to be too impulsive. Take your time in making a decision.

FOUR OF WANDS

Venus in the house of Aries signifies that a person's love life needs to find more of a balance. A loved one may be feeling neglected, used, or taken advantage of.

FIVE OF WANDS

Saturn in the house of Leo means that a person needs to stand up for themselves, find their inner strength, and be heard. They need to have confidence in their abilities.

SIX OF WANDS

Jupiter in the house of Leo brings good fortune, happiness, and a sense of pride in one's accomplishments. Don't get too pushy or arrogant, as fortunes are easily reversed.

SEVEN OF WANDS

Mars in the house of Leo shows that forgiveness is the way to move forward. Take a stand and show everyone who you are in life.

EIGHT OF WANDS

Mercury in the house of Saturn represents taking a chance and going one step further. Do not just settle; go the extra mile. Your enthusiasm and open communication will set new grounds in a venture.

NINE OF WANDS

Moon in the house of Sagittarius represents a need to be free and independent of current restrictions. To break free, one has to open up more and be willing to commit.

TEN OF WANDS

Saturn in the house of Sagittarius warns that having tunnel vision will stop you from seeing the big picture and taking advantage of all the opportunities out there.

THE KING OF WANDS

The King of Wands is associated with the element fire but has no direct astrological association.

The King of Wands tells of an overachiever who sets their sights high and is not afraid to climb to them. They like to be in charge of the workplace and are very artistic and/or creative.

QUEEN OF WANDS

Queen of Wands is associated with the element water but has no direct astrological association.

She shows someone who works hard and provides support for those in need. Her creativity goes a long way in helping others.

PAGE OF WANDS

The Page of Wands is associated with the element earth but has no direct astrological association.

A Page is a young man just reaching maturity and still has a youthful air about him. He is very skilled and hardworking but lacks imagination.

KNIGHT OF WANDS

The Knight of Wands is associated with the element air and has no direct star, sun or moon sign associated with the zodiac.

The Knight signifies a great quest or journey into self-discovery and a thirst for knowledge to gain more ground in the work environment.

ACE OF SWORDS

There is no astrological association. This card is associated with the element of air.

To move forward, you will need to be a bit more ambitious and let your curiosity guide you.

TWO OF SWORDS

The moon is in the house of Libra, which signifies that you may be holding yourself back due to unfounded fears and lack of confidence.

THREE OF SWORDS

Saturn in the house of Libra brings about a lot of discord and disharmony on the home front. You have been feeling rather detached from those you love lately, and it is time to sort things out or move on.

FOUR OF SWORDS

Jupiter in the house of Libra brings about a need for change in a relationship that is going through a very rocky patch. Ask yourself, is it worth fighting for or is it time to let go?

FIVE OF SWORDS

Venus appears in the house of Aquarius and brings about a new relationship that is a lot different from the ones you have had before. Let go and allow yourself to feel.

SIX OF SWORDS

Mercury is in the house of Aquarius, which is a good time to make travel plans, write exams, or ask for a raise. Don't lose sight of your goals as you transition into this new phase of your cycle.

SEVEN OF SWORDS

Moon in the house of Aquarius brings about a lot of emotional conflict, uncertainty, and a lack of self-esteem. Approach your problems head on, as it is a make or break situation.

EIGHT OF SWORDS

Jupiter in the house of Gemini shows that there is a lesson to be learned in your current situation. Until you have faced this and don't make the same mistake over and over, you will not move on.

NINE OF SWORDS

Mars in the house of Gemini represents a feeling of discontent, a restlessness in the soul and need to break free. Be very wary of making impulsive decisions right now or you could end up in hot water.

TEN OF SWORDS

Sun in the house of Gemini brings about changes that you are not ready for and warns of a person around you that will walk over you to achieve their goals.

KING OF SWORDS

There is no direct astrological link to the zodiac for the King of Swords, but he is associated with the element fire.

The King of Wands is a man of great wisdom who has achieved and/or accomplished a lot in his life. You can learn from his wisdom and should take his advice if you want to move forward in your life. He is also a very dominant figure, so take care if you are in a relationship with him.

QUEEN OF SWORDS

There is no zodiac representation for the Queen of Swords, however she is represented by the element water.

The Queen of Swords is a woman who is not afraid to stick up for those she loves. She is a fierce mother that will not stand for bullying. She is a provider, protector, and will challenge anyone who dares to get in the way of her loved ones.

PAGE OF SWORDS

The Page of Swords is represented by the element of earth and has no zodiac representation.

He is an enigmatic young man that has yet to mature but he works hard and has the potential to grow into his status.

KNIGHT OF SWORDS

The Knight of Swords is not associated with a zodiac sign but is represented by the element air.

He is a man with great ambition and will stop at nothing to get what he wants.

ACE OF PENTACLES

There is no astrological sign directly linked to the Ace of Pentacles, however it is associated with the element of earth. The Ace tells of the beginning of a more stable situation where there is a lot of potential if you are willing to work hard.

TWO OF PENTACLES

Jupiter is in the house of Capricorn and leads to good fortune but warns about overspending and to think before you buy. Do you need that, or are you just being greedy or a spendthrift?

THREE OF PENTACLES

Mars is in the house of Capricorn, which means that you will start to feel a bit more control over where your life is going. Take advantage of this new cycle you are about to enter, and you will find your self-confidence again.

FOUR OF PENTACLES

Sun in the house of Capricorn warns that now is not the time to retreat into an inner shell. Let your feelings be known and stand your ground. Let bullies know they will not be tolerated.

FIVE OF PENTACLES

Mercury in the house of Taurus brings about an upheaval that leaves you feeling unsettled and alone. Do not despair or be afraid to ask for help. It will be found with whom you least expect it.

SIX OF PENTACLES

The moon is in the house of Taurus, bringing about a very emotional time to show compassion for those in need. Do not be stingy with your material possessions. A friend in need is a friend indeed!

SEVEN OF PENTACLES

Saturn in the house of Taurus sees a person resistant to anything new and stubbornly refusing to even bend a little bit. Don't let your insecurities stop you from experiencing new things.

EIGHT OF PENTACLES

Sun in the house of Virgo represents great talent and lots of potential. Pay attention to the fine print in a contract and don't be afraid to take your time in going over things more than once.

NINE OF PENTACLES

Venus in the house of Virgo represents having to let go of your emotions if you want to move forward in a relationship. You can be with someone and still maintain your own identity and independence.

TEN OF PENTACLES

Mercury in Virgo brings about a learning curve in which you will be given a lot of great opportunities. Don't be afraid to ask for help, as it is not a sign of weakness.

KING OF PENTACLES

As with most of the court cards, the King of Pentacles is not associated with a zodiac sign but is instead associated with the element air.

The King of Pentacles is an enterprising and well-established older gentleman. He is mature, stable, and kind.

QUEEN OF PENTACLES

Queen of Pentacles is associated with the element water but has no direct astrological association.

People are drawn to her as she is beautiful, graceful, and nurturing. Her resourcefulness and intellect show a great business mind.

PAGE OF PENTACLES

The Page of Pentacles is associated with the element earth but has no direct astrological association.

The Page of Pentacles is hard working but not very responsible and lacks maturity. He needs to be grounded to achieve his potential.

KNIGHT OF PENTACLES

The Knight of Pentacles is associated with the element air and has no direct association to a zodiac sign.

The Knight signifies a man who is willing to take on the world for those he loves and/or is loyal to. He has overcome many obstacles and lives to fight another day.

ACE OF CUPS

There is no astrological association. This card is associated with the element of water. The Ace signifies that a new journey is about to begin and that you should make sure you are ready for it. You may need to tune into your intuition to take the initiative and drive forward.

TWO OF CUPS

Venus is in the house of Cancer, making this an emotional time where there will be a lot of ups and downs. Try being a bit more affectionate in your relationship. There is no harm in letting those you love in.

THREE OF CUPS

Mercury in the house of Cancer signifies that there is discord in the home front that needs to be addressed, or your happy home will soon become a stormy or very lonely one.

FOUR OF CUPS

The moon is in the house of Cancer, which makes a person's vulnerability come to light. Don't be afraid to share how you are feeling and get help addressing your insecurities.

FIVE OF CUPS

Mars in the house of Scorpio means there is someone in your life that is being a negative influence. It is time to clean house, use your charm to settle arguments instead of brute force, and try a little sensitivity in matters of the heart.

SIX OF CUPS

Sun in the house of Scorpio means that there is going to be a big challenge ahead. You may as well accept it, as the other path has just as many obstacles to overcome to move forward.

SEVEN OF CUPS

Venus in the house of Scorpio brings a new and very intense love. Make sure it is really what you want and or are ready for. Standing too close to the sun is sure to turn you to ash.

EIGHT OF CUPS

Saturn in the house of Pisces means that a sacrifice has to be made to achieve your goals. Have a little faith in those around you and let someone else takes on some responsibility. You cannot do it all yourself if you want to get ahead.

NINE OF CUPS

Jupiter in the house of Pisces means that now is a time to work on your compassion and open up your heart. You need to be a bit more sensitive to the needs of others.

TEN OF CUPS

Mars in Pisces means you are going to have a boost in energy and are feeling that things can be accomplished if you put your mind to it.

KING OF CUPS

King of Cups has no associated zodiac sign but is associated with the element fire.

A man of stature and wealth that wears it with ease but does not make an issue of it. His wisdom and knowledge make him a great person to listen to.

QUEEN OF CUPS

Queen of Cups is associated with the element water and has no associated zodiac sign.

She is a very maternal figure who will do whatever it takes to ensure the well-being of her loved ones. Her kindness is legendary, and she is associated with doing great charitable deeds.

PAGE OF CUPS

The Page of Cups is associated with the element earth and has no zodiac associations

A man that still needs to reach emotional maturity and one that is as yet not ready to settle down, as he still has a lot to accomplish in his life.

KNIGHT OF CUPS

The Knight of Cups has no zodiac sign associated with him, but the element of air is.

The Knight is a man that has fought many battles for those he is loyal to, but he is seeking enlightenment and way to move forward on his own.

CONCLUSION

It does not matter what deck you have chosen, as long as you feel comfortable with it. As a novice, it may take you two or more decks of cards before you find the one that you connect with. But, give your first choice a good chance before deciding to get another, as first impressions apply to choosing most things in life, especially with naturally intuitive and spiritually connected people.

Listen to that gut feeling you get when you know in an instant if you are going to connect with something or someone. When choosing your Tarot card deck, do not try and force the issue. If at first you do not find the deck, continue to look. Some people can make a connection over the internet, whilst others need to physically feel them. That is all a personal choice.

Just like choosing your Tarot cards, do not force your readings. At first, you will find that you will need to reference what they symbolize. But it is important to note that the symbolism can change a bit to adjust to the situation and where the card lies in the spread. Take your time to analyze different spreads and relax into it. Soon, you will be able to feel your way as your intuition grows and becomes fine-tuned.

As you started this journey with me, I introduced you to the connection of various other divination arts and how they work hand in hand. Never be afraid to delve into each of them, as the more you know about the spiritual realm and all the tools on hand to tap into it, the stronger you will become as a card reader. It will give your reading more depth and dimension if you can understand your subject on different levels.

Learning astrology, numerology, runes, and palmistry gives you a deeper look into the mystic world. The deeper you delve, the stronger your spiritual connection to the universe becomes. Another important art to learn would be meditation, as not only is it yet another way to get in touch with your inner self, but it cleanses the mind, body, and soul. It is very important to have that downtime and clear off any leftover energies and vibrations from intense readings.

Take care of your cards and try not to do one reading right after another, as you may find that you will not get an accurate one. Make sure the environment in which you are doing your readings reflects who you are and is one in which you are most comfortable. If you feel off balance or awkward, then it is going to come through in the readings, which is unfair to the person you are reading for. If you are having a bad or overly emotional day, it is best not to take readings for other people either.

Always clear your mind, relax your body, and let your troubles go when doing a reading for another. Make sure all your energies are concentrated on the subject before you let anyone else touch the cards. Soft lighting and/or even the gentle flickering bounce of a candle or two can create an atmosphere in which the questioner will feel soothed and comfortable.

If a person is coming to you for the first time, try remembering how you felt the first time you got a reading. Then proceed in the way you wished your first reading had gone or been done to make you feel more comfortable. If people feel comfortable with you, they will trust you more and with trust, they will begin to open up more, which in turn gives a more accurate reading.

The more people you can help and show the way, the more people will come to see the Tarot as a path to spiritual enlightenment. That the cards are there to guide and offer a different perspective on the answers or truth they seek. They are not magic, nor can they predict the future, but they can bring hope, shed light on the different options/paths available to them, and hopefully help them make better choices. If nothing else, the cards will give them some courage or a push to re-evaluate what they can achieve.

With this book, you should now have the basic tools to begin your spiritual journey into the world of Tarot card readings. The most important chapters in the book that you may need to go over more than once would be:

- Chapter 3 – The Major Arcana

- Chapter 4 – The Minor Arcana

- Chapter 6 – Reading Patterns and Interpretations

- Chapter 7 – Reading for Yourself

- Chapter 8 – Card Combinations

The above chapters give you the foundations on which to start building your reading interpretations. It is only through practice, patience, and determination that will you grow spiritually. Let your intuition guide you as you take what you have learned from this book and add it to the rest of your Tarot card discovery journey.

Learning the Tarot is not hard. Just like anything new it has to be practiced, and the time put into it is what you can expect to get out of it. Remember that you have the power to influence those you read for, and that is a great responsibility that should not be taken lightly. Like any artist, practice, practice, practice until you can confidently give yourself an accurate reading.

Practice giving readings to close family and friends before trying to read for a stranger or distant acquaintances. Never try to force someone to have a reading, as you have to remember that part of your journey is to show people that Tarot reading is not the "dark art" it has been made out to be, but a tool of divination that is meant to guide and offer support during a time of need.

Your journey has started along with your choice of Tarot deck, and armed with references like this guide, you are now ready to take the next step. Let the intuition of the Arcana of Cartomancy lead you through a discovery of love, success, and prosperity in your life.

BIBLIOGRAPHY

7th Sense Psychics. (n.d.). Guide to Tarot Cards [PDF File]. Retrieved from https://www.7thsensepsychics.com/tarot-book/TarotBook.pdf

Banzhaf, H. (2005). Tarot and Astrology [PDF File]. Retrieved from https://www.ta-rot.de/artikel/AstrologyTarot.pdf

Farley, H. (2009). A Cultural History of Ta-rot: From Entertainment to Esotericism [PDF File]. Retrieved from https://stilluntit-ledproject.files.word-press.com/2015/05/helen-farley-a-cul-tural-history-of-tarot-from-entertainment-to-esotericism-2009.pdf

Foster, S. (2015). The Tarot, Synchronicity and the Psychology of C.G. Jung [PDF File]. Retrieved from http://www.safoj.org/wp-content/uploads/2015/02/2015.03.21Fos-terCOLOR.pdf

Fra, G. H. (2012). Tarot Symbolism & Divi-nation [PDF File]. Retrieved from http://www.thelema.org/publica-tions/books/LiberT.pdf

Heart of Stars. (2016). The Minor Arcana [PDF File]. Retrieved from http://heartof-starstarot.com/wp-ontent/up-loads/2016/09/minor3rdedition.pdf

Jodorows, A., & Costa, M. (2009). The Way of the Tarot: The Spiritual Teacher in the Cards [PDF File]. Retrieved from http://tarothermeneutics.com/classes/Jodorowsky-Camoin/handouts/Alejandro_Jodorowsky_-_The_Way_of_Tarot.pdf

The Daily Tarot Girl. (n.d.). How to Read Tarot for Your Self [PDF File]. Retrieved from http://www.daily-tarot-girl.com/wp-content/uploads/2016/05/How-to-Read-Tarot-for-Your-Self.pdf

The end... almost!

Reviews are not easy to come by.

As an independent author with a tiny marketing budget, I rely on readers, like you, to leave a short review on Amazon.

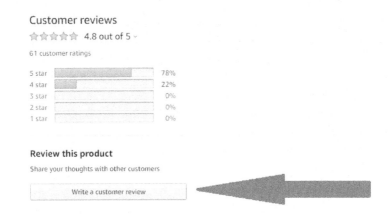

So if you enjoyed the book, please...

Leave a brief review on Amazon.

I am very appreciative for your review as it truly makes a difference.

Thank you from the bottom of my heart for purchasing this book and reading it to the end.